# SEVERING
# **SOUL TIES**

## APRIL D. WESLEY

**Severing Soul Ties**
Queenship Restored Publishing
ISBN-13: 978-0692859780 (Custom Universal)
ISBN-10: 0692859780

Printed in the United States of America

Scripture quotations taken from The Holy Bible, New International Version®NIV®
Copyright © 1973, 1978, 1984, 2011 by Biblica, Inc.™
Used by permission. All rights reserved worldwide.

"debauchery; discord; dissensions; drunkenness; envy; factions; fits of rage, hatred, ideal; idolatry; impurity; insecurity; jealousy; orgies; selfish ambition; witchcraft." oxforddictionaries.com. 2017. http://www.oxforddictionaries.com (7 January 2017).

Editing: Grace & Co. Editorial Services by Dominique Bozeman
Writing Services by Katrina Phiri
Editing Services by Emily Juhnke

Cover Graphic Design: Norbert Elnar at masterpiecemovement.com

Cover Original Artwork: Queenship Restored™ presents its second artistic collaboration with artist Serena Saunders. After accepting the invitation to create the cover art design for "Severing Soul Ties," Serena instantly devoted her time to studying the scriptures of Galatians 5 and Romans 8 to gain artistic clarity and direction for the commission. The interpretation is woman/man looking to God for the severing of their soul ties. The black butterflies (soul ties) are behind him/her. Transformation to God's Will happens with the colored butterflies, and true freedom is attained (severing soul ties) with the white butterflies.

# TABLE OF CONTENTS

# DEDICATION

To the person who thinks their sins are too significant, that God couldn't possibly think they're worth anything, or feels forgotten about (by God or man).

# BACKGROUND TO SEVERING SOUL TIES

## Chapter 1: Introduction to Soul Ties

When I was called to this task of writing about soul ties, I was elated but terrified. I couldn't help but think about all the issues that soul ties have caused throughout my life. The thoughts of them exhausted me, and thinking about how I would relay it all in a book exhausted me even more. But God, as He always does, reminded me that it would not be me writing the words but Him. Just like He taught me to recognize the bondage of soul ties and delivered and healed me from them, He also reminded me that His power could do it for many others if they allow (John 3:16).

Many introductions came to mind to open this book, but consistently and firmly God instructed, "Take them straight to the Word. Make it plain." Thus, His Word reads:

*"So I say, walk by the Spirit, and you will not gratify the desires of the flesh. **For the flesh desires what is contrary to the Spirit,***

*and the Spirit what is contrary to the flesh. They are in*
*conflict with each other, so that you are not to do whatever you*
*want. But if you are led by the Spirit, you are not under the law."*
*-Galatians 5:16-18*

*"The **acts of the flesh** are obvious: sexual immortality, impurity*
*and debauchery; idolatry and witchcraft; hatred, discord, jealousy,*
*fits of rage, selfish ambition, dissensions, factions and envy;*
*drunkenness, orgies, and the like. I warn you, as I did before, that*
*those who live like this will not inherit the Kingdom of God."*
*-Galatians 5:19-21*

*"But the **fruit of the Spirit** is love, joy, peace, forbearance,*
*kindness, goodness, faithfulness, gentleness and self-control.*
*Against such things there is no law. Those who belong to Christ*
*Jesus have crucified the flesh with its passions and desires. Since we*
*live by the Spirit, let us keep in step with the Spirit. Let us not*
*become conceited, provoking and envying each other."*
*-Galatians 5:22-26*

You may ask, how do these Scriptures relate to *Severing*
*Soul Ties?* Our souls, or our own spirits that live inside us,
constantly want to be connected to and fed by some
source. Just as we fill our physical bodies with food, our
souls (or spiritual bodies) experience similar desires to be
filled. Our spiritual bodies are either fed by God or Satan.
Plainly, this equates to the Spirit (ruled by God) or the
flesh (ruled by Satan). Thus, as Paul writes to the church
of Galatia in the book of Galatians, we are being
encouraged to thrive and receive nourishment in our lives
by the fruit of the Spirit, not the acts of the flesh. The
flesh leads to the denial of the inheritance of God, and the
Spirit of God grants direct access to all His inheritance

here on earth as it is in heaven. This is a very simplified explanation.

Yet, the origins between the two nourishing sources are rooted in an all-time spiritual battle. It is dictated in Scripture, *"For our struggle is not against flesh and blood, but against the rulers, against the authorities, against the powers of this dark world and against the spiritual forces of evil in the heavenly realms"* (Ephesians 6:12). What's interesting about the descriptors of the flesh and Spirit in Scripture is that the flesh is exactly that, happenings in the physical (flesh and blood). They are actually struggles that distract us from what our focus should be, which is the Spirit. Satan has used the acts of the flesh to numb and distract us from the concerns of the Spirit. Instead of us being used for love, joy, peace, kindness, goodness, forbearance, and gentleness to bless this weeping world, he'd rather us be gratified in the flesh. This not only brings our individual selves harm, but it brings others harm as well. The devil places his minions in our midst (the rulers, authorities, powers, and spiritual forces of evil) for our struggle to be obedient to God's Will. If we are confined to Satan's plots and plans, (our souls are tied to the ways of the flesh) we will be banished away from the Kingdom of God and join Satan in utter disarray and purgatory for eternity.

This is NOT God's Will for our lives. As we learn what it means to have a real relationship with the living God, we realize our true submission lies within what we choose to be filled with. He desires for His Will to be fulfilled in that we demonstrate all things of the fruit of the Spirit. This leads to His specific purpose created for our lives and for this dying world's needs to be met in, by, and through His

Spirit. If we do not sever our ties from sexual immorality, impurity, debauchery, idolatry, witchcraft, hatred, discord, jealously, fits of rage, selfish ambition, dissensions, factions, envy, drunkenness, orgies, and the like, we will stay tied to the enemy and his ways, plots, and plans. Every burden, life experience, question, and doubt should no longer be "aided" by the flesh but filled by the Spirit of God. This is choosing life over death.

*What is a soul tie?*

A soul tie can be a spiritual, mental, or physical bondage to people, roles and tasks, ideals, or material possessions. Soul ties are either Godly or ungodly in origin. Thus, they are either created and approved by God or used as a manipulation tactic by the enemy (Satan). An example of a Godly soul tie to a person is the institution of marriage, where one person is bonded to another spiritually, mentally, and physically as God has ordained and as described in the Bible. Another Godly soul tie can be to a role or task, such as the application of one's purpose. This could vary from being an educator, to opening up a consulting firm, to music production, or to creating a non-profit organization. Godly soul ties to ideals can include visions or dreams that are given by God through the Holy Spirit. These also often directly relate to one's purpose here on earth and confirm Biblical truths. There are no Godly soul ties to material possessions because they never contribute to our treasury in heaven (Matthew 6:19-21). Godly soul ties are God-ordered, and the unfulfillment of them would be considered disobedience to God. They

ultimately edify the Kingdom of God by bringing God's
Will to fruition.

Ungodly soul ties are one of the most plaguing reasons for
our lack of spiritual maturity and inability to understand
and apply the Word of God. These soul ties are the
ultimate forms of distraction and make the Word of God
null to the bonded person. Ungodly soul ties to people can
be familial or can involve obsessions and relationship
bondages to people that we aren't married to; or for those
that are married, this can involve placing a spouse higher
in importance than God. For roles and tasks, ungodly soul
ties are created when a position, role, or title is more
superior than the tasks created by and for God. Even tasks
that are rooted in God-given purpose can become ungodly
when they transform into idols of busyness and become
more important than one's actual relationship with God.
Ideals can be the most deceptive entity of ungodly soul
ties. Particularly in our media-driven world, we can
become bonded to the "idea" of something: the idea of
being the prettiest or most handsome; the idea of having a
surplus of money; the idea of achieving more degrees,
titles, or accolades; or to hit closer to home, the idea that
we are supposed to be in relationship with someone that
God has said no to. (We will touch on this later.) Plainly,
we are bonded to the idea of being our own god. These
soul ties consume every resource freely given to us by
God. Material possessions fall directly into this
consumption of ungodly soul ties. It includes any physical
object that consumes one's thoughts and motivation. We
are most known for being bonded to money, living
environments, vehicles, clothing, and other forms of
possessions. This list can go on and on.

*Why do they need to be severed?*

Any form of an ungodly soul tie attempts to disrupt the mission of the Blood of Jesus Christ. Ungodly soul ties must be cut off, severed. They are a complete disruption to and distraction from our purpose here on earth. We can remain in bondage for years due to engagement from corruption of the flesh. This is why we see years of generational strongholds. We mimic what we've seen over time and what is familiar to us.

Ungodly soul ties are sin.

*"In the same way, count yourselves dead to sin but alive to God in Christ Jesus. Therefore do not let sin reign in your mortal body so that you obey its evil desires. Do not offer any part of yourself to sin as an instrument of wickedness, but rather offer yourselves to God as those who have been brought from death to life; and offer every part of yourself to Him as an instrument of righteousness. **For sin shall no longer be your master**, because you are not under the law, but under grace. What then? Shall we sin because we are not under the law but under grace? By no means!"*
*-Romans 6:11-15*

*"Just as you used to offer yourselves as slaves to impurity and to ever-increasing wickedness, so now offer yourselves as slaves to righteousness leading to holiness. When you were slaves to sin, you were free from the control of righteousness. What benefit did you reap at that time from the things you are now ashamed of? Those things result in death! But now that you have been set free from sin and have become slaves of God, the benefit you reap leads to holiness, and the result is eternal life. For the wages of sin is death, but the gift of God is eternal life in Christ Jesus our Lord."*

*-Romans 6:19-23*

Severing equates to death because it cuts off the life source.

*"Do you not know, brothers and sisters - for I am speaking to those who know the law - that the law has authority over someone only as long as that person lives? ... So, my brothers and sisters, you also died to the law through the body of Christ, that you might belong to another, to Him who was raised from the dead, in order that we might bear fruit for God. For when we were in the realm of the flesh, the sinful passions aroused by the law were at work in us, so that we bore fruit for death. But now, by dying to what once bound us, we have been released from the law so that we serve in the new way of the Spirit, and not in the old way of the written code."*
*-Romans 7:1,4-6*

*"Therefore, there is now no condemnation for those who are in Christ Jesus, because through Christ Jesus the law of the Spirit who gives life has set you free from the law of sin and death. For what the law was powerless to do because it was weakened by the flesh, God did by sending his own Son in the likeness of sinful flesh to be a sin offering. And so he condemned sin in the flesh, in order that the righteous requirement of the law might be fully met in us, who do not live according to the flesh but according to the Spirit."*
*-Romans 8:1-4*

## Exhortation

The purpose of this book is to recognize the places of bondage that have created soul ties in your life, learn how to sever them through Jesus Christ, and properly heal so that you can truly live out your purpose here on earth. The devil has dwelled within our bondage for far too long. Now is the time to fully understand who God says we are in Him and be completely delivered from our soul ties.

I believe I was born and bred for this book. Actually, that's probably not true considering sin was never God's intention, but my experiences with the many soul ties I've encountered prove the Scripture true, *"And we know that in all things God works for the good of those who love Him, who have been called according to His purpose"* (Romans 8:28). God has allowed me to clearly see sin that creates ungodly soul ties, sin that allows ungodly soul ties to take root and harvest, and the many complications thereof. Most importantly, I've become a living witness to how soul ties can only be severed by and through the utilization of God's powerful and true Word available through the Blood of Jesus Christ. For there is no sin that cannot be undone through Jesus Christ. There is NO soul tie that cannot be severed if one says they truly believe and understand what the Blood of Jesus Christ has done.

*Prayer*

Lord, I pray that these words have already started to cut through the heart of each reader like a double-edged sword. The world we live in is faulty and manipulative, encouraging us to continue to live in and through the flesh, which is sin-filled. We've succumbed to faulty ways of the flesh through experiences with our parents, siblings, friends, associates, co-workers, media, possessions, and our own perverse mindsets. These ways will never inherit the Kingdom of God and allow righteous freedom. Help us to genuinely desire You, the understanding of Your Word, and have repentance in our hearts so that we will desire the Spirit instead of the flesh. We have gone the wrong way for way too long, and it has only bred mayhem in our lives. Take control, God. Teach us, lead us. Help us not to be like dogs that continue to return to their vomit (Proverbs 26:11). The flesh breeds death, but the Spirit breeds freedom and eternal life. Lead us in this journey. In Jesus' name we pray, amen.

## Chapter 2: My Story

It was August 20, 2011, the day after my graduate school commencement ceremony. I was excited, nervous, and still in major study prep for starting my new career in the coming weeks. I was waiting in the car, and I received a call. It was a Saturday. Once I said, "Hello," the lady on the other end stated that she was a nurse calling from my gynecologist's office. I'll say this, it is NEVER good to receive a call from the gynecologist's office during non-business days, especially after you just received a full panel of STD testing. At the time, I hadn't fully given up sex. For years, during the act, God would literally be speaking to me, telling me to stop, telling me that my body belonged to Him and no other person who hadn't paid the ultimate price for it, which is the covenant of marriage. I used to cry in the act because I knew my actions displeased God. It was so dysfunctional and unenjoyable.

On that day, as I heard the nurse say, "We've received the results of your test and y o u r   t e s t   w a s   p o s i t i v e f o r....," my whole life slowed down and every incidence of fornication replayed in my mind. I envisioned every time I was in bed with a person I was not married to, who was not my husband. I had not committed to anyone under God inside the sanctity of marriage, but I continued to, over and over again, give my body away for years. I felt like it had caught up with me and that I'd gotten what I deserved. She ended up telling me that I had contracted something that could be cleared with an antibiotic and proceeded to ask what pharmacy location I would like my prescription sent to. I stopped for a moment and began to cry. This was probably my third time being in this situation. Even as she said the words without revealing the results, I thought, "This is my third time. Whatever she says, I deserve it. I had it coming for me. I kept rejecting You, God, so I deserve it." My soul wept. God spared me again. At that very point, I told God, "I am so underserving. You are Holy. I will never again defile the body you have given me. It is my reasonable service. I will never have sex again until you entrust me to do so within the sanctity of marriage. I am Yours." I absolutely meant that at that time, and it has continued to be the best decision I have ever made.

While still speaking with the nurse and in the moments thereafter, I reflected on the people I had been sexually involved with and those they had been involved with. I began to realize the implications of those connections. Sex not only exposed my body, but it also exposed by soul to all of the issues within their souls. I then began to think of all the brokenness that I was dealing with as an individual and the additional brokenness I received with every soul that I was tied to because of my sexual partners' sexual partners. I began to see that my disobedience implicated more than just a decision to start doing the right thing. I would need to initiate a process to disconnect my soul from relationships it had been tied to, knowingly or unknowingly.

See, the reason sex was intended for a man and woman within marriage is because the issues between them, carried within their souls individually, are intended to be worked out and loved as intricately and delicately as 1 Corinthians 13 describes love to be. Those imperfections that are shared as souls connect are meant to be covered with the love of God as two become one, where the two can work out their salvation under God's covenant and provision. When soul ties are created from fornication, our souls take on issues from the sexual partner that were never intended for our taking. We are overtaken with soul connections that cause an addictive desire to be fixed. We perceive that this "fixing" can only be fulfilled sexually. This only creates a gateway for more sin. It leads to a soul tie cycle that leaves us wanting to be filled by something from someone that is unfulfilled.

As I received more issues from my partners spiritually through sex, the merging of souls through the flesh, I cannot neglect the fact that I was already filled with my own issues. Literally, I was struggling with everything from Galatians 5:19-21, *"Sexual immorality, impurity and debauchery; idolatry and witchcraft; hatred, discord, jealousy, fits of rage, selfish ambition, dissensions, factions and envy, drunkenness, orgies, and the like."* I was spiritually sick and engrossed with the flesh, the complete opposite of the Spirit of God. I had no idea of the spiritual consequences of these acts. I was wretched; wretched in my devotion, my heart, my mind, and my life. How did this come about? Where did the need to be loved and cared for so intimately come from?

My childhood was marked by considerable love and support from my family, most notably my mother, grandmother, and grandfather. Yet, as many women who seek love and attention in all the wrong places, my history with my father was not the best. My mother and father had a significant soul tie to one another that started when they were both nine years old and probably is still present until this day. From my understanding, they had a relationship off and on from their junior high years until I was sixteen years old, a relationship that spanned over forty years. Yet, they were never married.

As I described in my previous book, when I began to develop a relationship with my father at three years old, I never felt a genuine love like I felt with my mother. The best way I could describe it was that I felt tolerated by my father for the sake of him remaining in a relationship with my mother. This may not have been the feeling on his end, but it is definitely what I felt, even at that age. When my father would come over to our house, I sensed a love from my mother toward my father that was unexplainable. Considering my mother's general toughness, there were very few times that she seemed vulnerable, ever. Those times were mostly seen when she was with my father. She was smitten. He was, too, for her, but that was just it. They were "in love," and I just so happened to be their daughter. Again, this may not have been the case from their end, but this is what I felt throughout my childhood. As I grew up and sensed the lack of real commitment (marriage) that was never made to my mother and my father's lack of genuineness, integrity, and dedication in being my father, I became angry. I did not respect him. The only man I listened to and respected was my grandfather. He genuinely loved me and cared for me, not just in a financial sense, but he desired the best for me. He nurtured me and put me above his own desires. I never felt that with my father, period.

In reflecting on my father's situation now as an adult, I have realized he was only giving me what he knew to give me at that time. He was only giving my mother what he thought was decent, not realizing that he was demonstrating boyish ways in not being intentional within their relationship or in leading a family. Beyond my anger for his lack of commitment to my mother or never biblically leading our family, I was also genuinely saddened that he never treated me like a princess, what I thought the father/daughter relationship should look like. I wanted his validation; the type of validation that says, "No one is ever good enough for my daughter." I lacked and wanted protection, authenticity, and a genuine closeness. I was seeking agape love that only Jesus Christ provides. That was actually the real problem.

After my grandfather passed away when I was fourteen years old, I longed even more for what I felt was missing in me and my father's relationship. I seemingly found it with my first serious boyfriend that same year, to whom I eventually lost my virginity. This initiated a cycle in which

I was willing to do anything and everything to keep my relationship going so that I could continue to feed the insecurities and hurt in my heart.

From one boyfriend to the next, I continued to long and search for the same thing, agape love. I had every kind of boyfriend, from some who literally bought me whatever I wanted to those I would beg to spend time with me. The strong desire to be satisfied with love from a man was often paralleled with sexual immorality. It, too, eventually grew in my life. This one act of the flesh fostered and supported other acts of the flesh that began to grow in my life. The process of trying to gain an identity from finding love was actually causing the opposite to happen. I was losing myself almost to the point of death.

Years before the call on August 20th, the Lord had been speaking to me, telling me He was my only source of real love. My earthly father could NEVER fill the depth of love that only Christ gives. I thought that giving my all to someone, including by body, would be my atoning sacrifice, the representation of who I was and the extent I was willing to give. Yet, in actuality, there is only One atoning sacrifice, Jesus Christ. As humans on this earth, we can never give enough of ourselves to match what God has done for us or the extent of His love. This is why everything contrary to God's love and Spirit, the acts of the flesh, can never sustain us. It will literally leave us empty-handed and unfulfilled every time.

So what was my triggering point? What marked my final straw to turn to God? I would have to say that it was a true change in the position of my heart. I began to feel a love for God similar to what He had been feeling for me. I felt a longing to be obedient and to stop abusing His gifts. Little by little, I began to spend very intentional time with Him. I learned to pray, read my Bible, understand and follow His Word, hear His voice, and serve people and His Church. Most importantly, I developed wisdom and discernment for awareness of the devil's schemes and how he wanted me to stay connected to my soul ties. Again, for years, God had been calling me out of my sin, and I'd refused. This time, His overwhelming love reached me not to punish me even though I deserved it, but in a compassionate way. I couldn't go back to my soul ties. I began to learn why they needed to be severed. It made me uncomfortable and disgusted to think about returning to what God was delivering me from. It was my reasonable service to learn more about Him, serve Him, and develop a heart like His. Actually, I began to feel less bound and, instead, actually free in Christ.

The last five to seven years of my life have prepared me for this moment. This time has been spent in major spiritual growth filled with pruning, frustrations, learning who God is for myself, and observing His Will unfold in my life in His timing. It has shown me exactly who God is, that His Word never returns void, and that His promises are everlasting. Second by second, minute by minute, hour by hour, day by day, month by month, year by year, I've watched God encourage and honor my obedience by providing me more than I could have ever imagined. I've seen him totally restore and bring blessings into my life that many would say should've taken decades. Although the enemy tried to take at least a decade from my life that could have had consequences for generations, being obedient to God fast-forwarded gifts that were not only beneficial to living a life of righteousness, but that also ultimately were used to benefit His Kingdom. Please don't think the gifts that I'm referring to are people, relationships, positions, tasks, material possessions, or ideals. I'm speaking of the fruit of the Spirit and spiritual gifts (1 Corinthians 12:7-11).

Through this time of getting to know God and being obedient in severing ungodly soul ties, God has released me to share with others. Hence, the writing of this book. The Lord calling me out of a lifestyle filled with sexual immorality was ordained for this very moment. He is using my experiences as a medium to explore the other acts of the flesh that trouble His heart throughout this world. As I address soul tie issues in this book, with the Lord's direction, I will continue to divulge circumstances that have helped me to sever soul ties and ultimately receive and accept freedom through Christ. I am no longer bound. The most important thing to understand is that this is a process of allowing the Lord to take His time to peel off each layer of soul ties in your life. Of course, God can cause complete deliverance from all of our sins within a blink of an eye. Yet, in most cases, for sure in my case, His glory is shown the greatest through the actual process. Every time I rejected Him, every day of being disobedient, every year of wondering why, and every time I could say, "Thank you, Lord!" has allowed me to see who He really is: the Prince of Peace, Wonderful Counselor, and Mighty God (Isaiah 9:6). He is waiting on you to do the same.

I am no special person. I am just someone who said, "Yes!" to God. You, too, have the same opportunity and privilege. I pray that throughout this book, you are able to reflect on your journey and prepare to truly sever ungodly soul ties once and for all. I pray that you will latch onto God and seek His will and way for your life like never before.

# DEFINING SOUL TIES

## Chapter 3: Family

*Background*

Family (soul) ties are the most debilitating and bondage carrying of all soul ties. They can have the greatest generational impact and, thus, must be addressed first. Although I am not a psychologist or a family counselor, I believe God has given me discernment, insight, and wisdom in recognizing the stark debilitation of fleshly ties to family; most notably the relationships between child and father, child and mother, siblings, and other family members. Our current struggles with sin almost always have a direct correlation to what our upbringings were like, the stress that was evoked in those relationships, and the consequential spiritual uprisings or downfalls that happened thereafter.

The words and actions of our family can set the tone for sin's presence in our lives for a lifetime. Whatever is contrary to the Word of God, whether supported or refuted by your upbringing and the beliefs of your family, must be cut off. This is not to say that you do not continue to love your family, particularly in the unconditional manner that God loves us in spite of our sin, but our call as believers is to abide by His Word and live as examples of it.

The intimate connection we have with those we consider to be family creates our first soul ties with people. It consequently impacts the ways we see, perceive, acknowledge, and respond to sin. It is such an important soul tie to discuss because it is innate. The tie is built in the mother's womb and continues to flourish at birth. Our family is the first point of human (flesh) interaction that we receive in the world. They are referred to as "family ties" for a reason.

Family can be the best vessel for guiding loved ones to the saving grace of Jesus Christ, harboring love and righteous direction. On the other hand, family relationships, the associated upbringing, and the consequences thereafter have the power to dismantle our souls in a way that is unmatched since there is an authentic flesh and spiritual connection incepted at birth! Again, family is not a tie that you choose in life. You are innately born into it. This does not mean that you are spiritually owned by them. Remember, you were bought by the most sacrificial price through Christ. God calls us to be separated from this world no matter what, even if it means choosing Him over our own family. This goes for any familial tie from our parents, siblings, children, aunts, uncles, or cousins. Whatever we are tied to that keeps us bound and away from our rightful connection with the Holy Spirit must be severed. We are to be tied only to the Holy Spirit. Everything else should be put in its proper place and prioritized under God.

What does this look like with each family member? For our parents, we are to respect them and honor them as it says in Ephesians 6:1-4. Yet, they are not our god. Anything that has been said and done by them that has created an ungodly soul tie must be severed. This means we stay respectful to them, but we are under righteous law to God and not to anything they may say or do that goes against God's Word. For our siblings, aunts, uncles, or cousins, they are under the same pretenses. With our children, we must not make them an idol. They belong to the Lord first. Children are God's most precious gifts to this world. They are truly God's gifts. When you think about the women who petitioned God for children in the Bible, including Hannah and Elizabeth, they were so joyous for God's response to their prayers in giving them a child. Yet, their gift was an assignment by God to birth and care for the children for His use. The ultimate purpose of Samuel and John was to be used mightily by God for His Kingdom. This is the mindset we must have with all people; they don't belong to us, and we don't have ultimate control over them just as they don't have ultimate control over us. They, too, are purposed for the work of God and not directly for our benefit.

In our upbringings, we have observed and participated in sinful behaviors that were considered acceptable and normal. These behaviors have consequently become a part of our lives as ungodly soul ties. Because childhood inhabits our first learning experiences, what we learn during this time often molds our perceptions for receiving and responding to all behaviors. As we come into the knowledge of the truth through Jesus Christ, it is our duty as Christians to identify and break all behaviors that oppose the Word of God.

In contrast, Godly soul ties to family are described in Ephesians 5 and 6, the chapters that are the guidelines for Christian households. We must *submit to one another out of reverence for Christ*" (Ephesians 5:21). All actions and beliefs that reside in the family dynamic should be done out of reverence for Christ. Anything that opposes reverence for Christ should be considered an ungodly soul tie.

*Application*

So what are some common forms of ungodly soul ties that we see in families today? We see parents who have put themselves before their children and are not submitting to one another out of reverence for Christ. This creates hostile environments within the family due to anger, rage, and being disjointed and unengaged. This is perceived as neglect to the child, and the child eventually seeks acts of the flesh to fill the void.

Another commonality seen is the lack of a mother and father working together to raise the family as stated in the Bible. Even if the parents do not operate in the same home (maybe due to death, divorce, or mutual agreement), the goal should always be to raise the child in the ammunition of the Lord and not in a spirit of being malicious to the other parent or child. The children can naturally pick up these spirits of dissensions and factions. This eventually causes a lack of peace in the child's life and an inability to have healthy relationships. Another commonality with ungodly soul ties in the child-parent relationship is the observance of fornication or any other forms of sexual immorality and impurity. To the child who may have seen multiple men or women go in and out of the home throughout their upbringing, this breeds confusion and a lack of stability. These are just a few examples that represent actions and consequences within the dynamics of family soul ties with parents.

In an effort to really address the various examples of brokenness caused by family dynamics and ties, I thought it best to discuss some family scenarios that I've experienced as well as examples from family and friends. The goal is to help you identify and uproot ungodly soul ties that have caused a lack in your life and encourage you to fill those empty places with the fruit of the Spirit instead of the acts of the flesh. I pray that you will allow the Holy Spirit to open your heart to places that have impacted your soul, where you have hardened your spirit from receiving God to heal that area from your family situations and experiences. I pray these scenarios will bring awareness to those hidden areas and awaken the need to address the soul tie that has kept you in bondage for far too long. Our family soul ties can be the hardest to get rid of because they have been there the longest, and we have learned to adjust and hide the issues skillfully.

We have adapted to our dismantling and impurity at heart created by insecurities, bondage, and disdain from our family. The enemy loves this. He wants us to stay broken and feel burdened and heavy-laden. But God says, *"Come to me, all you who are weary and burdened, and I will give you rest"* (Matthew 11:28). Let's start the process of willfully uprooting your family soul ties and laying them down at God's feet, never to be picked up again.

<u>My Personal Experiences:</u> My personal experiences of living completely for God and refuting my fleshly desires to live in "comfortable sin," as was supported by my upbringing, started when God called and separated me completely from my family. Sometimes, the best way to start the severing process from ungodly family ties is to separate yourself physically. This should be done in a healthy way, of course. I was called by God to follow Him just as Abraham was called to leave his family to pursue the plan God had for him. I knew then and totally realize now that it can be difficult, but when purposed by God, it is for great reason. This, too, was applicable in Abraham's case where he completely separated himself from his family at seventy-five years of age. God had Abraham leave Ur of the Chaldeans (believed to be modern day Iraq), where his family worshipped the moon as their god (Joshua 24:2). Clearly, his family's ways went against serving the only true and living God.

I'm sure it was difficult to leave the only ties he'd always known, but when you are called by God, it's always worth the sacrifice. After being called and then severing his soul ties to his family, he initiated a journey of faith and obedience that encourages all believers to this day. This, too, is what we've been called to, but we have to first recognize what needs to be left behind and severed completely. The place God is bringing you to will always birth fruit and life instead of death. In Abraham's case, the benefits of his obedience to leave modern day Iraq is apparent to this day.

When God called me into separation from my immediate family, I was deciding about where I should go to graduate school. There was divorce happening, my mother and grandmother were in a tormented place in their relationship, and I had not seen or spoken with my father in more than five years. No one was seeking God in how to address all of our issues. I was constantly motivated to keep living for myself and focus on my independence. Yet, God was calling me to break the ties of selfishness and disorder that had occurred for so long in our family. Hatred and discord had caused our current situation. Because we didn't love and honor God, our hearts were rooted in the flesh with dissensions and factions. We were going nowhere fast. God called me to be completely separated from that.

Aside from changes in geographical location, He would direct me in when I should communicate with my family. At the time, my graduate program required intensive study and focus. I could not afford to be distracted by news about police investigations, the stress and worries from my mother and grandmother, or all the additional drama that was alive and well within my family. I couldn't continue to expose myself to that through communication with them regularly, and God gave me peace about it. As time went on, He also showed me that my family was a part of the world; I would just need to learn and know how to separate from it. When He asked for my undivided attention, it meant that I had to put away all ties that were not from Him, completely separating myself (severing them).

From this process, I began to learn what it truly meant to be separated from the flesh. Every act of the flesh that you can fall into from a family issue can be mended if you tie yourself to the Spirit of God. If you allow yourself to trust God with your issue for long enough, He will properly discern to you the way; through the fruit of the Spirit, that freedom can come. That's why communication and trust in God is so important with severing soul ties. God knows the history of the issue, the sins that have been birthed from it, and the root situation that has led to your current reality. We must allow God to start the foundational changes necessary for severing these types of soul ties, as he did for me with physically moving.

To be clear, I'm not advising anyone to "run away" from their families if God has not told them to relocate. When God has given me clear instructions to do any geographical relocation, He has literally created the provision for it. That means He gave me the peace to move forward first, then the money, job, opportunity, etc. This is not something that should be on a whim or taken lightly. This is one of those situations where "you know, that you know, that you know" you're supposed to move.

Also, God sometimes has to separate you from your family so that you cannot be used as an excuse for their disobedience. God will have you leave so that He can be direct with them and they can never have the excuse that they didn't hear the Truth from God. Their denial of God will have to be to God Himself. In conclusion, our parents and all their issues, including ungodly soul ties, belong to God. Let Him handle them.

My Daddy Issues: After writing my first book, I thought I had finally come to a pinnacle of overcoming what I perceived to be my "daddy issues." I thought that I exposed everything that I still had within me until a friend responded to a comment one day saying, "That would be your response because you know you have daddy issues." Time stopped. I was in utter confusion because I didn't recognize that as being the case. In my mind, I no longer had daddy issues. My father and I don't have the ideal or picture perfect relationship by any means, but we have been working toward a better relationship. We speak at least once a month and tend to have decent and reflective conversation during every call. We don't see each other often, but we've only been in communication for the last three years after ten years with no communication whatsoever.

I was content in the relationship that I had with my father at this point. Yet, what my friend spoke was truth. There were dissensions and factions in my soul still present toward my father. A deeply-rooted place of unforgiveness, frustration, disdain, and hurt was present, and I hadn't **fully** let it go. This presence allowed the devil's work to continue to go forth in my heart. It was a place where I could easily pick up those moments of his mental and spiritual absence in my upbringing and then birth insecurity and frustration to my life. I kept giving the enemy power not only to be in control of the situation way back when, but also to continue to birth new life from these acts of the flesh in my present day. Only through seeking the Holy Spirit to empty me of those iniquities could I truly be free. Thus, when there is a trigger of the pain, hurt, and other emotions that I once kept inside, I am no longer affected. Through Jesus Christ, I've been released of needing to choose sin to feed my situation. I trust His Blood to cover what I thought I needed to cover on my own. I am free and no longer bound to what I believe my father should have done or to the insecurities and expectations I had developed.

A Loved One's Family Ties: Her daddy issues were very different from mine. This is a loved one who literally received whatever she wanted from her father. She had every toy, piece of clothing, food, and upkeep expenditures available at her fingertips throughout her childhood. What she didn't have was reassurance that her father loved her unconditionally. The possessions were oftentimes an "I'm sorry" gift for the names she was called and the abuse she witnessed. The mental abuse eventually caused her to seek the unconditional father's love from boys and men, creating a deeper hole in her heart and hardening it to God. She pursued the acts of the flesh when only the fruit of the Spirit could provide everlasting fulfillment. On the other hand, beyond being spiritually neglected by her father, she was also mentally and spiritually neglected by her mother. Again, an innate soul tie incepted at birth was attacking her ability to connect to the fruit of the Spirit. These issues have literally plagued her entire life.

The truth of the matter is that both of her parents had issues of neglect from their parents. Do you see how the devil will keep up these antics from generation to generation to ruin what God has intended for one generation to the next? It is on her at this point to choose deliverance over her family and the ungodly soul ties that she has been exposed to and submitted to. The defining change in her situation is declaring who God says she is over what her parents say that she is. This is the difference of knowing in her heart, through the fruit of the Spirit, that she is beautifully and wonderfully made instead of accepting the names from her parents like "stupid," "too big," or "ugly." They are only calling her what they view themselves as, nothing more. They, too, can be restored through the fruit of the Spirit.

If you know someone in this position or have overcome it yourself, you must keep encouraging them along the journey. This generational behavior and mindset must be severed at its root so it won't be passed along to the next generation.

My Friend's Family Ties: My friend had opposing views and responses from each one of his parents during his upbringing. His mother was extremely supportive and encouraged him with every fiber of her being. His father, on the other hand, was not present in his life or his siblings' lives for the majority of their childhood. He was exposed to his mother having a couple of boyfriends and one husband while his father was in and out of the home. In addition, his grandfather and other family members used verbiage that would blatantly separate him as physically incapable of doing certain tasks as well as verbally separate him from belonging to the family. He grew up always feeling that he had to prove his worth to his father and grandfather, secondary to apparent favoritism. He had a natural, innate desire to be accepted by them. To this day, he struggles with acceptance, often overcompensating with his availability to be present and capabilities to perform tasks just to receive their affirmation. This has led to major insecurity soul ties where he has to constantly affirm himself in Christ and overlook what was spoken over him through his childhood and even in adulthood. To this day, he constantly fights saying "yes" to every request just to seek affirmation for his very livelihood.

Unfortunately, this is a major battle that so many fight, particularly men. Because of these ungodly soul ties of rejection from childhood, insecurity overwhelms them in their development as men and hinders them from being all God has called them to be as leaders. Consequently, men seek the acts of the flesh to fill the voids created with insecurity and abuse. It is often not spoken of, but it's the truth. Men and women have to rise above the lies of the enemy. We must recognize and sever those deeply-rooted places where we have heard and believed the enemy's lies through our families. It's our only way of living the fruitful lives that we've been called to.

So, if you suffer from neglect or overall insecurities brought on by a family member and are now seeking affirmation, know that their ability to fulfill any of these things will never suffice in the way that God can. They are temporary beings, which physically assisted in the presence of your life here on earth, but they were not meant to sustain your life. Your existence and purpose are not dependent on them. Their purpose was to physically assist you in life, to teach you (whether that was done well or poorly), and even to be taught by your example. No matter what you've endured from them, you are not their words. You are not their actions toward you. You do not have to submit to your flesh to "heal" from their behaviors and actions any longer. Again, the acts of the flesh bring death, and the fruit of the Spirit brings life. You have been dead for too long. It's time to let go of the death in man. Your life has been awaiting the freedom found in Christ. Family will eventually die, but Christ will always live from everlasting to everlasting. Who would you rather be connected to?

*Reflection*

I pray that reflecting on these examples has illuminated some ties that need to be severed in your heart. It is so easy to tuck them away, ignore them, go on with our lives, and leave them to be dealt with at a later time.

Any of these examples could have applied to other family members not explicitly described in the scenarios above. The most notable biblical example of overcoming ungodly family soul ties is found within the story of Joseph. Joseph was a favored child in his household among his brothers because he was born in his father's old age. His brothers were jealous of the favorable love he had from their father and his ability to have and interpret dreams. Joseph was rejected by his brothers, kidnapped, sold, lied about, and thrown into jail. He was then restored and put in charge over all of Egypt after all the disdain, pain, rejection, and insecurity that he could have submitted to and allowed to take over his life. God knew that all of this would happen. Over and over in Genesis 37 to 42, it was stated that God was with Joseph, no matter if he was being sold, if he was enslaved, or if he was reigning over others. This is the same for us. No matter what bondage was intended and caused by our families, through Jesus Christ, we have the power to overcome and sever those soul ties. No more excuses.

We are waging a war against years of mental and physical mutilation from people, most notably our families. It has shaped our very responses in every part of our lives as adults. For example, the father who may not have validated his daughter or son with affirmation or physical touch during their upbringing could have caused the child to now have issues with associations, friendships, or romantic relationships as an adult. Or, the father could have grown up with the same issues previously mentioned, causing him to exhibit continuous anger to his son and/or daughter with brutal speech, physical abuse, or consistency between the two. Or, fathers and mothers could be choosing to neglect their children or sexually abuse them in order to gratify their perverse fleshly desires.

No matter your current situation or past experiences, you are not them. You spiritual body was not intended for the sin that has caused such disruption in your life with detrimental consequences. You and those you have ungodly soul ties to are intended for more than what the devil has equipped you to be within his workshop.

The truth is that this subject matter is extensive and cannot all be addressed in detail in this book. If this chapter has brought attention to places and spaces within your life that have not been thoroughly dealt with and you know that an ungodly soul tie is looming, you need to find solutions to sever it. I pray that you will seek wisdom from God through prayer, fasting, or any other preferred spiritual discipline to receive healing. We will talk about deliverance later in this book, but everyone's situation is different. Beyond an individual and spiritual approach with God, for accountability reasons, it may be advisable to seek a Christian counselor or psychologist to help you stay unbound. Whatever your choice is under God's leading, seek His absolute peace in your deliverance and in severing any soul tie that you need to with family or anyone else. I am praying for you and standing in agreement for your deliverance from all ungodly soul ties to family.

*Prayer*

Father, I pray in the name of Jesus that You will sever every ungodly soul tie to our families that we have submitted to. It is not of You, God. You sent your Son, Jesus Christ, to cover every sin and iniquity that we have experienced on this earth. We have been given the authority and power to overcome any act of the flesh. This is Your Word, Lord God, and we have the expectation of deliverance when we release it all to You. I pray that You will lead us in the proper spiritual equipping and resources to make this a lasting change so that we will not pick it back up.

I pray for the women and men who have endured such agonizing circumstances that leave them disjointed from purpose and effective relationships. Lord, I pray that You will give them timely reminders of who You've created them to be and that their circumstances and experiences will no longer dictate them. I pray for divine healing over their lives in Jesus' name, amen.

## Chapter 4: Friends and Peers

We often are unaware of soul ties that can be created with friends, peers, and associates. These groups fall into the relationships that we encounter at the workplace (managers, colleagues, co-workers); school (teachers, peers); friends; and other associates or acquaintances. In this era, we have become severely bonded to the words and actions that people tell and show us. We carefully consider their opinions, and they drive our daily decisions and actions. This applies to the words we say, to the way we dress, to our plans for school and work, and astonishingly even to dictate our purpose.

Giving anyone honor and control over your life as if they are God is idolatry. Following someone's motives, thoughts, and actions, and favoring their opinion above God's is idolatry. Any decision or action that is not God-driven is idolatry. People bondage, as we will speak of it in this chapter, describes humans as our god and lord. Our response to this bondage is participating in the act of the flesh, idolatry. Our goal as believers is to please God in every decision and action we make. He should be our only motivation, guiding light, and hope. People are never these things.

## Friends

Friends are often considered the family that we choose in life. We have the opportunity to create and maintain relationships with people that hold us accountable, love us unconditionally, and uplift us. A friend is supposed to stick closer than a brother. If you have friends in your life who do not meet the above definitions, they are not likely to be a true friend. A real friend should not persuade you against the Word of God, but rather they should encourage you to it. God-ordained friends encourage you to be exactly who God has created you to be, look how God has created you to look, and do what God has created you to do.

If you have friends who encourage you to compare yourself to others, don't encourage your worth in Christ, define themselves based on what's popular in media, and are generally more harm than good, they are not your friends. You are unequally yoked. As Amos 3:3 says, how can two walk together unless they agree? This means you cannot be unequally yoked, even in friendships, because one is dragging the other back, hindering the ability for the two to walk alongside each other and essentially inhibiting the other from going forward. Hearing, receiving, and doing actions that are encouraged by an ungodly friendship soul tie can be such a deadly, unwavering force that can inhibit your purpose for decades or even a lifetime. They must be severed.

The Unequally Yoked Friends: I've had several types of "friendship" situations from which I've been able to learn the difference between Godly and ungodly friendships. One was a friendship that I'd had since high school and ended in my early twenties. This friend supported me and engaged me in our relationship as long as her needs were being met. If I didn't give her the attention or involvement that she desired in the way she desired, she would often speak negatively to me or would have very jealous behaviors. Yes, jealousy is often between opposite sexes; but in this case, it was not. In addition, she often lied and was manipulative and extremely confrontational. This is how our friendship ended.

Although I was very hurt from it all for quite a while, it showed me what manipulation looked like: feeding on another person's spirit, no matter the level of sacrifice, in order to meet the needs and desires of the manipulator. Again, this is completely ungodly and disordered. One person is attempting to move forward in the likeness of God while the other is intentionally dragging them down and slowing down their process. This is the exact plight of the devil, to drag you down or cut you off at the neck completely, opposite the two oxen that are initially yoked together. We must be aware of the enemy's schemes in every "friendship."

The "Stop and Go" Yoked Friends: Another type of 'friendship" is one that is present and supportive in your endeavors rooted in God (as you are for theirs); however, they are constantly and repetitively dealing with the same struggles. Over time, they've demonstrated an inability to completely sever those soul ties they've suffered from, including some that you might have been delivered from. You love them, you've known each other for years, and you care for each other deeply, but the truth of the matter is your relationship heavily involves you coming to their rescue about repetitive soul ties. This is the type of relationship where you are walking together, but you have to constantly pause on your path because the other ox is sick and you have to aid or care for their situation before you can start along the path again.

As brothers and sisters in Christ, God calls us to walk alongside and uplift our fellow brother and sister throughout this life. Yet, God does not call us to be infected with what they're infected with. See, because we are walking so close to them, observing their situation, hearing their speech, and being closely connected to their actions, it's easy for us to pick up what they haven't let go of and any sicknesses that may be slowing them down. This could be the friend who we've known and walked with for years; they could be proclaiming their commitment to God, but their actions are of the flesh instead of the Spirit.

I'm not saying to quit on these friends; I'm saying to guard your heart, spirit, mind, and body from infection. Pray for them, intercede for them, and give them wisdom as the Lord leads, but don't get infected. All it takes is a small cut in your flesh (from a wound that was previously closed) to re-open and spread like wildfire. Think about the situation as being re-engaged in a sin you've overcome, yet your friend is still suffering in it and won't sever it. Because you keep trying to pick them up and save them, you, too, get engulfed within the sin. It starts to look comfortable to you, and now your millimeter cut or exposure to your flesh has become a mile and you're all the way exposed and infected again! The devil is out to steal, kill, and destroy, and he just looks for a little crack! We must stay on guard by renewing our minds daily in preparation for every way that the enemy is trying to take us away from being engaged to the Spirit and get us to resubmit to the flesh.

Equally Yoked Friends: A Godly friendship is one that is not easily broken. It is not exhausting; it is exhilarating. It is one that is stern with accountability. Its purpose is to keep you on the path to what God has called you to do. It is equally accountable, meaning you both rely on each other to do and say what God would say and do, no matter how hard or uncomfortable it may seem. The byproduct of Godly friendships is the forward progression of God's purpose manifesting in each one of your lives. Each person is able to receive from the other because they know it is from good motives and intentions. All relationships can experience disagreements or difficulties at times, but at the heart and spirit level, each person in a Godly friendship knows that the other's actions are necessary and of the Spirit. Godly friendships produce the fruit of the Spirit instead of the actions of the flesh, always and in all ways.

*"And we urge you, brothers and sisters, warn those who are idle
and disruptive, encourage the disheartened, help the weak, be
patient with everyone." -1 Thessalonians 5:14*


### School and Professional Peers

Whether in high school, undergrad, graduate school,
corporate America, medical professions, private business,
or entrepreneurship, the pressures associated with these
opportunities have become overbearing, to say the least,
in today's society. We are constantly listening to and
filtering through the opinions of peers, educators,
mentors, managers, and other people that we encounter in
these institutional worlds.

Throughout our lifetime, encountering these major
influencers can cause both positive and negative
consequences in our lives, in particular to our spirits, if we
are not careful and sensitive to them. The spirit of
comparison is rampant. You are compared in scores, rank,
or position for an end goal. Receiving and applying the
advice of a colleague, counterpart, or other associate
(peer) has been the hallmark of discontentment in the
lives of so many. We have become bonded to the words
and actions of peers, just as described in the friends
section. Godly and ungodly peer bondage can have the
same descriptors as above.

We are not to be defined by the trend in professions and
suggestions for job choices and schools. We must not be
bound to the opinions of man, ever. The more we submit
to man's opinions, even with school and work, the more it

drives the spirit of comparison to think that we are not good enough, that we haven't done enough, or that we haven't achieved enough, whether personally or in comparison to a group. The fleshly desire to satisfy others based on their opinions leads to sin. We submit to idolatry, hatred, discord, jealousy, selfish ambition, dissensions, factions, greed, and envy. We abandon the opinion of God and manipulate our flesh to produce the results that this world wants.

The enemy will use peers within school and the workplace, mentors, and teachers to lead you away from Christ and His Will for your life. The enemy can be most deceitful in stressful situations. Stress causes apprehension, poor focus, and anxiety. The fruit of the Spirit cannot inhabit this space. This is why it is so important to have wisdom about who and what you receive from. The moment you start to feel inadequate because of the opinions of peers and institutional situations, the flesh takes over and the Spirit is discarded. Be sensitive to the Holy Spirit in what you receive from people. Allow the Lord to lead you in every detail of your day, particularly in your interactions with people in these settings. Be influenced by what the Holy Spirit is leading you to do and not what man is encouraging you to do, especially when you see that their motives are inspired by the acts of the flesh.

### Social Peers

One of the biggest culprits of people bondage in today's society has to be the spirit of comparison we receive from media, especially social media. No matter your age group or background, there are visual cues and verbal reminders to compare yourself constantly, and the enemy hopes that you would feel the need to compete. The enemy is trying to filter his manipulation and deceit and make it appear as if it cannot be harmful, even when we know that it can be and can consequently separate us from God.

Women study media, admiring what we perceive to be the perfect hair, the perfect waist, the perfect shape, the perfect clothes, and most of all, THE PERFECT MAN. Ha! What a lie of the enemy; the manipulation! Do you know that the enemy is the father of lies and manipulation? Because of this, he will burn in hell. That, too, is where our bondage to these images and social fantasies need to go. We have no room for this foolishness any longer. Our souls are at stake from a matter of fantasy.

Men, you are in the same boat. The spirit of comparison is running so rampant amongst you for what is considered important, but God considers it all idolatry. Men, you cannot look to the right or the left for what you should be doing and should have; you must look up! Your life and worth are not defined for the amount of money you make, the degrees you hold, the clothes you wear, your account status, or the beauty of the woman you attain, as portrayed by many forms of media. You are defined by your obedience to God's Word, period. Obedience to the Spirit has eternal benefits and is so much better than any highlight reel.

Stop looking to the right or the left and being inspired by what is temporary. Nothing will qualify or have longevity unless it sets itself up for an eternal position.

Men and women, stop looking to the media for direction in your life. As you can see, media is notorious for loving one person in the morning and hating them by the afternoon. Why would you feel comfortable in following something that is so fickle? This mindset is the enemy's; it breeds confusion and inconsistency, which in turn leads to fixing the issues with the acts of the flesh. Again, we are back in a continuous wheel of bondage that never ends unless we sever it.

In conclusion, there are major consequences that plague our society due to ungodly soul ties to people. It's not that the spirit of comparison or feelings of inadequacy have emerged just from media sources or that people are now worse than individuals of yesteryear, but we now have a more effective means of exposing the sexual immorality, impurity, envy, jealousy, and debauchery due to our current societal resources.

Today, make a decision to stop being degraded by and bonded to people, succumbing to the pressures, and replaying things said and done by friends, associates, teachers, professors, peers, colleagues, and managers. As men and women of God, we will no longer be stifled in our spiritual growth. We will no longer submit to finding solutions for our needs with acts of the flesh. Our ties have been severed. Freedom is found through Christ Jesus.

*"Do not be misled: 'Bad company corrupts good character.' Come back to your senses as you ought, and stop sinning; for there are some who are ignorant of God-I say this to your shame."*
*-1 Corinthians 15:33-34*

**Chapter 5: Insecurities**

Insecurity is a soul tie birthed from the enemy and supported by lies. Oxford defines insecurity as "uncertainty or anxiety about oneself, a lack of confidence, or a state of being open to danger or threat." Insecurities are self-doubts, rooted in fear. Just as the definition in the second sentence describes, insecure spiritual beings are uncertain about who they are, lack confidence within themselves, and are therefore open to threats from the enemy. Insecurity consciously lives up to the enemy's lies and is in absolute defiance to what God has called us to be.

When we feel insecure, we tend to "shrink back" and succumb to the opinions of others, comparison, and other lies of the enemy. Insecurities feed our soul ties because our self-doubt tells us that we need something or someone other than God to make us whole. Thus, we depend on relationships, material possessions, ideals, or tasks to fill our insecurities instead of identifying who Christ says we are in His Word.

We suffer from insecurity because worldly validation is often our identification. We feel we must be validated to have worth. This is a distraction and tactic the enemy uses to make us think that God's creations are never good enough. The only validation we need is the truth of God choosing us.

*"To this you were called, because Christ suffered for you, leaving you an example, that you should follow in his steps." -1 Peter 2:21*

This means that our goal is to live like Christ and not according to the world's standards. This is our guiding light and directional compass.

What is our motivation for succumbing to the trends, being flashy, and desiring to be looked at and regarded with a label? Our society is more pompous and self-centered than it's ever been. Men want to be regarded as being able to provide a fantasy of sorts (money, cars, clothes, etc.). Women, frankly, are in competition with themselves. We desire to see what we can do next in order to ultimately outdo others. The devil has us highly deceived! This continuous desire of want stems from an emptiness within ourselves, one that can only be filled by God. Our souls are tied to the envy, greed, and jealousy that have us hooked! Our insecurity is the inability to be who God has made us to be. We rely on who the world says we are.

What do we really need to be insecure about? How much easier would it be to rest in God, to nullify our flesh, and to eternally feed our spirit?

*"For the foolishness of God is wiser than human wisdom, and the weakness of God is stronger than human strength."*
*-1 Corinthians 1:25*

*"Brothers and sisters, think of what you were when you were called. Not many of you were wise by human standards; not many were influential; not many were of noble birth. But God chose the foolish things of the world to shame the wise; God chose the weak things of the world to shame the strong. God chose the lowly things of this world and the despised things - and the things that are not – to nullify the things that are, so that no one may boast before Him."*
*-1 Corinthians 1:26-29*

If we profess to be believers but submit to insecurity, we are essentially calling out the Word and God's promises as lies. These corrupted thoughts are parent thoughts of all the other small insecurities, such as appearance or comparison. We succumb to and feel defeated by our fears because we believe the enemy's lies over God's truths. Society supports these lies. As servants and disciples of the most high God, we must start submerging ourselves in God's Word instead of the enemy's little whispers. This will be our saving grace and aid us in severing all soul ties related to insecurities.

*"They stumble because they disobey the message - which is also what they were destined for."*
*-1 Peter 2:8*

*"Live as free people, but do not use your freedom as a cover-up for evil; live as God's slaves. Show proper respect to everyone, love the family of believers, **fear God**, honor the emperor."*
-1 Peter 2:16-17

## Chapter 6: Dating Relationships

*The Cycle*

As you have read in previous chapters, my soul ties to the
men I was involved with over a ten-year period not only
involved physical bondage, but, most detrimentally, they
also involved spiritual bondage. Where I thought I longed
for just sex, my soul actually was yearning for spiritual
contentment. Spiritual contentment can only be achieved
with the fruit of the Spirit filling the soul. It cannot be
achieved by acts of the flesh, including sex and other
forms of sexual immorality. The quicker this is understood
in our minds and hearts, the faster men and women can
be released from sexual soul ties and become whole
through Christ.

Sex before marriage in a dating relationship is not the answer. To be clearer, no forms of sexual impurity (oral sex, masturbation, pornography, fantasies, etc.) are going to provide the spiritual contentment that your soul longs for. If you can be honest, think about the guilt, shame, disgust, frustration, and worry you end up feeling after partaking in each act of the flesh. I know firsthand the feelings of being disappointed in my actions. I even thought that God could not use me and that my continued disobedience was too much for Him to change and make new. The devil is truly a liar!

God has such great plans for you! I will tell you that if you are currently reading this book, God wants you to be free from any impurity. It does not honor Him. God wants you to have righteous perspective so you will be without excuse and have the opportunity for all of your ties to be severed. The amazing thing about severing soul ties in dating relationships, or for any soul tie for that matter, is that Jesus Christ has already won the victory for us to go forward in Godly direction more than two thousand years ago. The enemy wants you to believe a lie that God's power is dead and cannot overcome your shortcomings. Well, I'm a living witness that He can!

After being involved in a ten-year cycle of submitting to soul ties in my dating relationships, my breakthrough came one day when my heart finally mourned what I had been doing to God. I realized that my flesh didn't matter because it would one day return to dust. My soul would live forever, and there were two options for its placement. I said, "Yes!" to God and to never turning back to that sin. As believers, we have the authority to live righteously because of the sacrifices made through Christ Jesus. He gives us both authority and power to say no to dating relationships that do not honor Him, to say no to getting involved with any sexual impurity, and to abstain from any sexual temptation.

My deliverance from the soul ties of my dating relationships happened after my last sexual encounter. I remember going home, lying next to my bed, and just frantically crying, so much so I had a headache from all the physical exertion. I remember calling my close friends and literally crying to them over the phone. They couldn't really lend me true comfort because they were not the Comforter that I needed. As I've said before, God had been petitioning me to leave my relationship that was filled with lust and not His love. He allowed the arguments, the frustration, and the sexual encounters so that I could see that nothing would change. I had been saying, "Yes!" to a vicious cycle that had me bonded for years. My soul, being continuously petitioned by the Holy Spirit, had enough. It was actually longing for God, because God had His hand on me.

## The Declaration

My sisters and brothers, soul ties to dating relationships are killing us one by one, whether we realize it or not. We are zombies, being controlled by music, movies, family history, encouragement from friends, etc., that encourage our behaviors and commitments to sin in dating relationships. Each time you say, "This will be the last time" or "I'm only going to see him or her one more time and that's it," you are just reopening a revolving door unless you cut it off. I know by experience. I did it for at least two more years after being broken up from my last relationship. At times, it can take double the time to sever the soul tie, so why prolong the process? God is able to restore, as the old saints say, what the cankerworm has taken from you (Joel 2:25). Even if you feel you've wasted an extended amount of time by dragging along your obedience, God can speed up your process of being fully restored in Him if you just say, "Yes." If you do not sever it, it can and will continue for the rest of your life.

And don't think for one minute that God is willing to bless your mess. For example, don't pray for a dating relationship that He has explicitly told you to leave. Let that man or woman go! I pursued God in my relationships only as a means to foster and "bless" the relationship. Let me remind you now that God created you; He is aware of any seed of manipulation you're trying to use Him for. If God does not want you be with someone, you will not be with him or her. If you continue to pursue a relationship knowingly out of His Will, you *will* be miserable until you say a final "yes" to God and initiate the process of severing that soul tie once and for all.

I used to pray and beg God to allow my ex and I to stay together. I just knew for a fact that he was God's best for my life and would be the one to whom I would be married. Well, God did not agree with the catastrophic plan I put together. This is not to say that I was dating a horrible person, but he was not God's best plan for my life, period. I wasted so much time on illusions, creating a scenario in my mind that was birthed from the flesh.

Soul ties in dating relationships begin because we don't know our identity in Christ. If we did, we would think twice about how easily we give up our bodies, which are our spiritual temples. It's more than a body exchange; it's a soul exchange. Literally, every issue that is within the person you give your body to is being exchanged and received within you during sexual encounters. Even in simple conversation, if you are not guarding your heart, ideas and thoughts can be received within your soul that plant seeds to feed and set precedence for desiring the flesh instead of the Spirit of God. The more the flesh is fed, the more the Spirit withers.

*"The body, however, is not meant for sexual immorality but for the Lord, and the Lord for the body. By his power God raised the Lord from the dead, and He will raise us also. Do you not know that your bodies are members of Christ himself? Shall I then take the members of Christ and unite them with a prostitute? Never!* **Do you not know that he who unites himself with a prostitute is one with her in body?** *For it is said, 'The two will become one flesh.' But* **whoever is united with the Lord is one with Him in spirit.***" -1 Corinthians 6:13-17*

In my dating relationships, seeds were planted first with thoughts and ideas of "what it could be." Physical connectivity seals these thoughts with emotional illusions that trick your body into thinking that you are receiving the "love" that your spirit needs, actually creating confusion to your soul. Your soul will continue to desire this fulfillment that will never happen. Thus, we can get so entangled in this illusion of a man or woman completing us, especially during the act of sex. This is a complete lie and trick of the enemy. The only time that sex can be truly edifying to the body is when it is done under the ordinance of God in a marriage. Otherwise, you are disrupting and corrupting any ordinance and relationship with God from disobedience in the flesh. No matter how many sexual partners are encountered, where the flesh is longing for a pinnacle of satisfaction, the soul will continue the process of being hooked to broken relationships with no goal or purpose. The soul will continue to desire an illusion if God's truth is not recognized and put into action.

This spiritual disarray will tag along even into marriage if the spirit is not caught as a single person in a dating relationship. We are called to guard our hearts. *"Above all else, guard your heart, for everything you do flows from it"* (Proverbs 4:23).

*"Flee from sexual immorality. All other sins a person commits are outside the body, but whoever sins sexually, sins against their own body. Do you not know that you bodies are temples of the Holy Spirit, who is in you, whom you have received from God? You are not your own; you were bought at a price. Therefore honor God with your bodies." -1 Corinthians 6:18-20*

### Breaking the Ungodly Soul Ties in Dating/Courting Relationships

Now is the time that we break the ungodly ties that are connected to our spirit (our soul) from being with a person in a mental, physical, and obviously spiritual way, knowing it produces no spiritual fruit. Remember, spiritual fruit is the fruit of the Spirit that includes love, joy, peace, forbearance, kindness, goodness, faithfulness, gentleness, and self-control. None of this is produced when you're in sin.

The infatuation with dating relationships is a major idol, distraction, and goal for the saved and unsaved person in today's society. In the unsaved, the desire for a dating relationship has a goal of fulfilling the emptiness within one's soul as described previously. It is a fulfillment that can only be achieved by God. Labels such as "relationship goals" are used to describe what we perceive as wholeness when we see couples that have the illusion of completion. I believe this is one of the enemy's main tricks and deceitful plans, to plant seeds in our hearts that we are not enough. The enemy plants seeds that a relationship with God is not necessary and does not complete you. The devil is a liar.

For the saved person, courting relationships have become the ultimate idolization even in having a relationship with God. We think manipulatively, as I once did, that having a relationship with God buys me the blessing of having an eventual courting relationship. We can go for years, hoping and praying that our relationship with God purchases our genuine desire for completion in the flesh, instead of the spirit. We actually get to a point of believing that God doesn't know we are attempting to use the Spirit to achieve a goal of the flesh. All idols, all things that we put above God, are known by God and will burn up before the judgment seat. We can't fool God.

In both scenarios, for the saved and unsaved, the solution is the same. In order for us to be fulfilled and know who we are, our worth, and our and value, Christ is the answer. What our souls yearn for in the flesh will bring us nothing but a continuation of lies and emptiness.

Let's cut to the chase. You don't think God can give you anyone better than the relationship you currently have or desire? You've made every excuse in the book for holding onto this relationship. "We've been together for years, and I've invested so much in my relationship. I need to stay with him because, truly, I might be the only 'god' he has in his life. He was committed to God before. He's just going through a rough patch, so I'm just going to have faith and stick it out." Wrong. Wrong. Wrong. The only righteous waiting is how God waits on us to FINALLY get it together and leave these worldly bonds that take us away from Him. His waiting for us shows an unconditional love. He sacrificed before the sin was committed in the flesh. It's the only waiting that heals instead of making us weary.

We need to allow God to be God. If He has truly ordained a relationship, we can let the relationship go and allow Him to bring it back full circle if He wants that for our lives. If not, being whole and committed to Christ means we have no worries and are not mad at God if the relationship does not return in our favor. God is a jealous God and desires for our hearts to be steadfast on His Will, even if it doesn't match our plans. This is the struggle for the saved and unsaved. Our flesh has to die in this so that our soul can finally live, wholly in Christ.

When a dating relationship soul tie is finally severed, the boundary is clear; they don't belong to us, and we look at them literally as our Godly brother or sister. We have a clear understanding that they belong to the Lord first, in everything. So, if that person finally allows God to change them from the inside out and God sees fit for them to become the spouse of someone else, you are genuinely excited for them and can even pray for a fruitful marriage for them and their God-appointed spouse. That's what a severed soul tie to a dating relationship looks like. Your soul no longer longs for that person but for God. You are inhabited with the fruit of the Spirit instead of the acts of the flesh.

## Being Single

We cannot negate the fact that being alone with God and severed from dating soul ties changes your status to being completely single. Godly singleness is a state of oneness with God, having no distractions from other potential relationships.

Unfortunately, being single with no accompanying dating soul ties is almost viewed as being accursed. It is not uncommon to be looked down on by people, including the saved and unsaved, because you are no longer entertaining purposeless relationships. Being in a state of singleness means giving undivided attention to God and allowing Him to prune and develop you for His purpose.

Let's discuss several situations that I've experienced in the enemy's attempt to keep me away from severing my dating relationship soul ties and truly being one with God.

Situation 1: As previously addressed, I was in a dating relationship for four years. It took two more years after the official "breakup" to completely rid myself of this person. God was petitioning me the entire time that I needed to be with Him and not the person that I idolized. One day, after another unsuccessful argument, I finally started to get it in my head that our relationship was just not meant to be. We didn't talk until three months later. (We had gone without talking for three months on several other occasions, obviously being unsuccessful with ridding the soul tie.)

After the three months, we decided to do a "final meeting" where the goal was to bring "closure" to our relationship. If I could insert an eye roll here, I would. I want you to know that severing a soul tie does not require a final meeting or closure. Those opportunities of communication will only widen small openings to your soul through a wound that is still not completely healed. The enemy loves to attack these places because he knows your healing is a process, and he can attempt to get in any crack or crevice that is a gateway to your soul. He wants your soul to continue to belong to him and not to God. That's exactly what happened to me. After seeing my ex for the final time, we continued to have random discussions over texts and occasional calls for an entire year.

Situation 2: The enemy also likes to work on your heartstrings when you've finally made a decision to be completely devoted to God and get rid of those dating soul ties. I would reach out just to "check on him," to alert him when a friend or family member passed away, or to share a joke that we used to laugh at, essentially to reminisce. For others, the challenge may be birthdays or special occasions that you once shared together. Whatever it is, don't allow the enemy to reopen a closed door. It's not worth it. He will always use guilt to lead you back into that person's presence and cause you to communicate with them one more time. I reassure you that it is all deception; the enemy wants you to stay in bondage, tied to that person forever, if allowed.

Situation 3: Another trick is that the enemy will convince you that you and your ex can be friends. Lie! You will convince yourself of that because when your ex gives you details of his new relationship, you provide advice thinking you no longer care about them and you've officially moved on. Lie! At some point, you are going to reminisce about what your relationship could have been with that person, and you will start to desire it again. Every emotion that you thought you've locked away will surely re-emerge, and you're now caught back in the matrix! Do you see how deceptive the enemy is? He roams around like a lion to seek whom he can devour (1 Peter 5:8). We must stay on guard at all times!

Situation 4: When you've finally made that decision to be completely single and not interact with the person you've been bonded to, you may also get tested from their end by them still attempting to reach out, have simple conversations, and get an overall response from you. Don't fall for it! My ex would text me monthly. He was the first to send me happy birthday wishes the day of my birthday, along with an accompanying Scripture. Don't fall for the enemy's tricks. Now, I don't believe that my ex had the heart to deceive me in all of this, but the enemy will try to use whomever he wants in order to keep you away from what God has called you to be. You must choose seeking God and keeping your eyes on Him no matter what's comfortable or "the right/nice thing to do."

Situation 5: The last time I met up with my ex for our "final talk," he expressed to me that he had a girlfriend whom he was planning to marry. Now, moving forward, why would I even need to entertain a man who clearly has been told by God that he is supposed to marry his girlfriend? As those who are seeking to sever a dating relationship soul tie and walk in true singleness, we need to have enough self-respect to be respectful toward the other person's new relationship. Meaning, if this man is telling me that he has a girlfriend he's planning to marry, I'm going to have enough respect for God, myself, and the other relationship to no longer interfere. He needs to be creating healthy, Godly ties with his new relationship. Even if he still wants to speak with me, I'm going to have enough respect for his new relationship and most importantly myself to be completely done and not give in to any advances. That's another marker of being severed from a soul tie. You want success for that person spiritually as well as for their future relationships. You want to ensure that you are playing no part in disrupting God's plan for their lives.

Pursuing Christ wholeheartedly and separating yourself from any dating relationship will require you to literally die to yourself, your old ways, the visions that you had for that relationship, and everything in between. You are laying your life down completely to start anew. It will be difficult most days at the start of the process, but again, you have to remember that God has given us the power and authority to overcome our flesh and operate in the Spirit.

An important concept I've learned in my experiences is that the enemy would like to lead you into depression because of your despair. Now, it is totally normal to be sad or even angry about where your life has gone, but you cannot wallow in it. Wallowing in what you have lost is just a tactic the enemy tries to lead you in so that your flesh can take precedence. This is the exact opposite of what God desires. He wants your spirit man to develop and your flesh to die. We have to take ahold of our situations and realize that it is more important to honor God, get away from this perpetual cycle, and finally live a life purposed for God, instead of being attached and unfruitful to man.

## Chapter 7: Marriage

Wow! This chapter has been pressed upon my heart in such a significant way. God has given me a spirit of insight into the way the enemy has planned to continue to plague families of ungodly soul ties through marriages. One thing that has been made clear to me through several confirmations is that the enemy is out to steal, kill, and destroy ALL marriages. Yet, the AUTHORITY and POWER of God through His mighty Word has overcome all the enemy can only wish to do. The enemy is roaming around like a lion seeking whom he can devour. Yet, the enemy has no bite when the Spirit of God inhabits a marriage.

A marriage is the physical and spiritual illustration and manifestation of God's love to human kind. It represents the joining of Jesus Christ to the church and how He gave himself up for her so that we might be saved (Ephesians

5:25). Genesis 2:24 also speaks of how a marriage is the uniting of two spirits as one flesh. This is the foundation of Godly soul ties in marriage and the reason the enemy persists in defiling marriage and making it ungodly. The enemy wants to take away every pure element of marriage, the fruit of the Spirit, and destroy it with the acts of the flesh. The acts of the flesh are ALWAYS the reason for the dismantling of marriages.

Separation and divorce in marriages are consequences from the acts of the flesh taking precedence over the fruit of the Spirit. At least one of the two spirits entwined has chosen this. The enemy just needs one compromised spirit, one that has a small crack in its vessel. If you give him a millimeter, he strives to take a mile. He will try to inhabit every nook and cranny of a spirit (one spouse) and ultimately infiltrate with sexual immorality, impurity, debauchery, idolatry, witchcraft, hatred, discord, jealousy, fits of rage, selfish ambition, dissensions, factions, envy, drunkenness, orgies, and the like. Yes, all of these acts of the flesh can be apparent in marriage just as they can in singleness. Don't be deceived.

Whether you are single, courting with intention of marriage, or in a marriage, please be aware of and equipped for the many schemes the enemy has to plant or maintain ungodly soul ties within marriage. Godly soul ties in marriage are described in Ephesians 5. It is completely reminiscent of and founded upon 1 Corinthians 13:4-8. Yet, ungodly soul ties in marriage are so cunning. The ability for the ungodly soul tie to form and persist is truthfully dependent on the individual souls present prior to the joining as one. If there is a crack in the foundation, eventually the house will shift. According to the testimonies and experiences of many of my married friends and associates, the condition of one's foundation prior to marriage is the defining reason ungodly soul ties manifest and persist in marriage.

For the focus of this book and chapter, we will discuss two very prominent issues of ungodly soul ties that appear to consistently attack the intent and purpose of marriages today. One, where a spouse has a pre-existing crack in the foundation, exposing the marriage to the possibility of an infiltration of any of the acts of the flesh. Two, the issue of idolizing your spouse. Both of these issues are major gateways for the destruction of marriage, family, and ultimately the Kingdom of God. They must be severed in Jesus' name.

### A Crack in the Foundation

A crack in the spiritual foundation of an individual within a courting or marriage relationship sets the foundation for an ungodly soul tie being created in the marriage. This allows the opportunity for any act of the flesh to infiltrate and inhabit the relationship. Let's explore some examples of this.

If there was a pre-existing spirit of lust that had not been dealt with completely, that can re-emerge in marriage. The pre-existing crack gives the devil the opportunity to introduce presentations in the person's midst that open the crack a little larger each time until complete destruction conveys. From here, each spouse can be exposed to the acts of the flesh that include impurity and sexual immorality, such as pornography and adultery. The person becomes intoxicated with lust, which inhibits their ability to make sober-minded decisions regarding their relationship and causes them to totally neglect the Word and Will of God within their marriage. The enemy has established a hold on so many marriages through this crack and its consequences. We must stay on guard!

Another example of a crack in the foundation is when a spouse is still tied to other men/women from past relationships. In the choice of engaging in marriage, the spouse could have thought that being married to someone else was the best method of getting over that old soul tie, but it was not. Marriage amplified the desires of satisfying the flesh from the old soul tie, and again, impurity and sexual immorality often commence because of this.

The idea of being with the "other person" does not die down in the spiritual body, and the desire grows for the old soul tie. This is why men and women get caught engaging in private phone calls, checking social media, and getting information from associates about their previous soul ties; their soul is still tied to another person while being married to their spouse. They actually are not one flesh with their spouse; they are joined with another as well.

This is also to caution the other involved party. They, too, are now tied to someone who does not belong to them physically or spiritually. They are married! We will address this further in another chapter, but it is all manipulation and corruption from the enemy at his finest. The spouse that is still bonded to the other person will have significant difficulty in mentally and physically connecting with their spouse because they are still spiritually connected to someone else. Arguments ensue because the spouse knows there is a disconnect, but they don't know why. All the while, the spiritual adulterer essentially has two spouses. This is reminiscent of the woman at the well who Jesus pointed out to have five husbands (John 4:7-26).

### Is Your Spouse Your god Instead of God?

Truthfully, do you idolize your spouse? Does your spouse give you ultimate satisfaction? Are you complete as a person because of the presence of your spouse? If you answered yes to any of these questions, you are fully submitted to idolatry of your spouse, which is an act of the flesh. This is not God's Will for marriage.

> *"Do not worship any other god, for the Lord, whose name is Jealous, is a jealous God."*
> *-Exodus 34:14*

A marriage is always supposed to have purpose; it is not meant to satisfy the flesh. The Will of God in marriage must be so purposeful that it outweighs the purpose of each person during their time as a single. Marriage is equipped for purpose as one unified spirit and for the production of new little spirits (children). All in all, marriage is meant to build up the Kingdom of God.

Thus, you are within an ungodly soul tie if you are only connected to your spouse through a piece of paper, a ceremony, and your flesh. God is not in it because He is not prioritized, your spouse is. The enemy can recognize this from a mile away and take you even further from knowing Godly intent through the fruit of the Spirit.

If you have married someone for the sake of having someone or because it was "time to get married," you are outside the Will of God and involved within the acts of the flesh. Ask God to give you righteous correction and direction in your marriage. Our desire should never be to solely satisfy the spouse and leave God out to dry. God is the priority, and a spouse is therefore prioritized under God as His Word states for order in the Godly household. We love and care for our spouses because we love God and are obedient to His Word. We don't love God as a byproduct of loving our spouse. That is disordered thinking and the foundation for an ungodly soul tie.

### In Conclusion

A common denominator with ungodly soul ties in marriage is that people don't know their identity and worth in Christ prior to getting married. The equipping and preparation for marriage happens long before there is a manifestation of an earthly spouse. It happens within the development of our marriage to God as a single (Isaiah 54:5). Through Christ, we receive the Holy Spirit who leads and teaches us how to be completely delivered and severed from any pre-existing soul ties and how He is the most important factor in our lives.

Anytime a mere human seeks validation from a person more than from God, they are already in a dangerous soul tie zone and out of Godly order. Validation from man, whether married to them or not, will always become stale and run dry. Only through the affections of God can one ever feel complete, even within a marriage. Being indulged to anyone more than your heavenly Father will always leave you within ungodly soul ties and distracted from your purpose, which should be your primary focus on this earth. We have enough zombies in this world; we need more marriages focused on purpose rather than on how each spouse can gratify the fleshly desires of the other.

We must no longer be half healed in marriages. People both engaged to be married or already married MUST be whole as individuals prior to the marriage and within the marriage. Wholeness does not equate to perfection or "having it all together." Wholeness means that God is Lord over their lives, that they choose to walk in His ways, and that they do not choose to run to a man or woman to fill a space that only God can fill. There is a major difference. Being whole also means living out God's Word and not submitting to the flesh, severing any previous ties of the flesh.

Releasing and being completely delivered of soul ties from people, especially with previous sexual partners, prior to or within marriage is paramount and must be done in order for the marriage to be fruitful. (In a later chapter, we will discuss how to cut off these soul ties.) I can't tell you how many marriages I've observed that have been distracted by old soul ties. It is detrimental for every person involved. Prayer must be performed with an acknowledgement of the issue, and the person must actively choose God over the acts of the flesh every time the enemy extends the opportunity. Don't despair; deliverance can take place and ungodly soul ties can and will be severed in marriages.

Marriage is too important of an entity to continue to allow the enemy to have his way over it. Individuals in a marriage must choose God now, or the enemy will steal, kill, and destroy it from every part of its weaknesses (soul ties).

*Prayer*

Lord, we pray right now for the severing of all ungodly soul ties within marriages in this world. We are aware of the enemy's plot to steal, kill, and destroy, but we will rely, depend, and stand on Your Word that has the power to dismantle every plan specifically projected on marriage. We rise up in Your power, given to us to overcome every plan of the enemy and completely restore marriages.

Lord, we pray for the man or woman who is still connected to another man or woman from a previous relationship. We also pray against the desires for lust and pornography that reign in this world today. We pray that You would cleanse the hearts of those in marriages from the inside out, so that they will be pure and desire Your Will and Way only.

We pray that You are always the priority in all marriages and not the sheer fulfillment of the flesh. We pray that the

Body of Christ never grows stagnant in praying for these issues because the Kingdom of God is at stake. We thank You that You hear us and are changing the hearts of many as we say this prayer. In Jesus' name we pray, amen.

**Chapter 8: Ideals**

As we established in the introduction of this book, there are Godly and ungodly soul ties linked to our thoughts or ideals. According to Oxford, the definition of an ideal is "a standard of perfection; a principle to be aimed at." Its synonyms are paradigm, prototype, conviction, and ideology. Meaning, an ideal can be a standard or a fixation of truth that we incorporate into our lives and fully intend to live up to because we are convicted of it. Now, beware that this is the world's definition of an ideal.

When we read the word "conviction" as believers, we know that true conviction comes from the Holy Spirit petitioning us to change. Thus, the world's definition determines a false standard, whereas the Godly definition of conviction warrants true and righteous change that merits holiness (John 16:8,13).

This is an important truth to establish early on because this is where the enemy tends to link our ungodly soul ties to our ideals, causing us to think that his way is the "standard" or correct way of thinking. In actuality, it breeds false hope, lies, manipulation, and deception into our lives. We can spend years trying to recover from a lie that the enemy has placed in our hearts regarding what our life should look like or who was intended to be in it based on the world's standard.

Let's dig a little deeper.

### How Are Ungodly Soul Ties Related to Ideals?

Being tied to ideals can make us wholeheartedly convinced that we are supposed to have a certain appearance, profession, relationship, house, children, picket fence, etc. I, too, have experienced being tied to an ideal; I planted a seed in my own mind about a potential relationship that I desired to be involved in, with the goal to marry someone that God never ordered or approved of me being with in the first place. I created a vivid ideology, from our first date, to meeting each other's parents, and to where we would move to after marriage. Because I allowed my flesh to be in charge, the Holy Spirit eventually checked me with finding out that he was actually courting someone else.

Ideals are usually very much self-evoked (guided by the flesh) and can seem innocent to think about, but they can cause great spiritual consequences. This is just one example of how an ungodly soul tie to an ideal can manifest in our lives if we aren't careful. We should constantly examine every thought with, "Is this God's desire or the enemy's deception?" Note: Just a quick answer; God gives peace and the enemy gives some type of uneasiness, always.

Ideals become our convictions, unknowingly tying motivation of the flesh to our souls and thus creating ungodly soul ties. In Western society, one ideal commonly referred to is the "American Dream." It is what's ingrained within us at an early age, and it includes the "criteria" of being an upstanding citizen and the quintessential order in which our lives should go. There's a formula given to every person: go to grade school, make good grades, go to college, get a degree, start a career, get married, purchase a home, have children, retire, assist with the grandchildren/ travel, and then die.

A preacher I know says, "The American Dream is a Christian's nightmare." We can have this ideal, this desire or vision for our lives based on the world's standard, but the origins often tie our souls to a direction that was never intended and directed by God. A lot of the made-up messes and circumstances that we find ourselves in are direct byproducts of an ideal that we latched onto and made an idol out of, and now our souls are bound to it. When we think about it, there are many areas in our lives that we've probably latched onto without God's direction. We now find ourselves in grave disappointment because the ideal never manifested.

You read these descriptions and may think that saying, "Your soul is bound to it," is too aggressive or dramatic, but it's true. Anything that you value greater than God is an ungodly soul tie, period. Our society has capitalized on our souls being bound to anything except God. We like to live in "never, never land" based on media, the opinions of our families, comparison, fear, and insecurities. We believe we have no value unless our lives mimic what's popular or meet the ideals of society. These are all lies from the pit of hell. Satan wants you bound to any and every ungodly ideal soul tie there is out there.

### Biblical Application

Discussing soul ties as it relates to society's standards or ideals reminds me of the story of Leah and Rachel in the Old Testament. The jealousy and struggle about what each woman felt to be ideal in their lives provides a transparent look at how an ideal can enrapture your soul and contribute to dysfunction in your household. The focus of this story starts in Genesis 29:16. Jacob arrives to an area called Paddan Aram and starts to work for his uncle Laban. Laban had two daughters; the oldest, Leah, and the youngest, Rachel. *"Jacob was in love with Rachel and said, 'I'll work for you seven years in return for your younger daughter Rachel'"* (Genesis 29:18).

After the seven years, Laban deceived Jacob, giving him Leah instead of Rachel, and Jacob was summoned to another seven years of work to receive Rachel. It was not customary at the time for the younger daughter to be married before the older daughter, so Leah was given to Jacob first. Then a week later, he was given Rachel in exchange for an additional seven years of work to Laban.

Now, there is no indication in the Bible that describes Rachel's affections for Jacob during his working/waiting period or her frustration thereafter, but I would assume she likely began to paint a picture in her head of what her life with Jacob would look like while he intentionally worked for her. Like many women who become soul tied to an ideal, she likely envisioned her story of being married and bearing children (the standard for women during their age).

Leah, on the other hand, was very insecure in her relationship with Jacob because she knew that Jacob loved Rachel and not her. As a way to satisfy her ideal and make up for the lack of love and sincerity in their relationship, Leah bore Jacob six sons of her own and an additional two sons through her servant Zilpah. Her ideal bred jealousy, competition, and hatred toward Rachel. As previously mentioned, Rachel, too, was soul tied to what she perceived to be important, bearing children from Jacob and having a family.

*"When Rachel saw that she was not bearing Jacob any children, she became jealous of her sister. So she said to Jacob, 'Give me children, or I'll die!' Jacob became angry with her and said, 'Am I in the place of God, who has kept you from having children?'"*
*-Genesis 30:1-2*

These two verses alone are power-packed, extracting the root of the real issues and consequences of ungodly soul ties as it relates to ideals.

Ideal Issue #1: Being tied to an ideal breeds the acts of the flesh. In Rachel's case, she was brooding with jealousy.

She even demonstrates fits of rage when she gives Jacob an ultimatum by saying she'd rather be dead than not have a child. Being tied to an ideal could make you lose yourself and your sanity. You are not sober minded because you are not led by the Spirit.

Ideal Issue #2: Rachel was so overwhelmed that Jacob had to remind her that she had lost what her true focus should be on, which was God. Rachel was obsessed with being married and bearing children. She was spewing out her anger for God's Will for her life on someone who had no control over her situation. Rachel was convicted that she was to have children just like her sister, but it was a worldly conviction, rooted in comparison and jealousy. If she had been seeking God, she could have been more at peace instead of anxious about her childbearing status.

*"Then she said, 'Here is Bilhah, my servant. Sleep with her so that she can bear children for me and I too can build a family through her.' So she gave him her servant Bilhah as a wife. Jacob slept with her, and she became pregnant and bore him a son.'"*
*-Genesis 30:3-5*

Ideal Issue #3: Like Abraham's Sarah, Rachel felt the need to take the situation into her own hands, worsening her already complicated family situation. She gave her servant to Jacob as another wife, who bore two more children. Can you see how jealousy, dissension, and factions can be birthed from just an ideal? The enemy was able to infiltrate their situation and create such a web of chaos and confusion.

God eventually allowed Rachel to birth Joseph, who became one of the greats of the faith in the Old Testament. Yet, how did this early presence of idealism work against their family dynamic? Remember, Joseph's brothers sold him into slavery. As we've seen in the story of their parents, his brothers were birthed from hearts of idealism. They, too, eventually conceived and birthed the same acts of the flesh, jealousy, envy, greed, dissension, and factions (that drove the evil behaviors eventually demonstrated to Joseph). Do you see how the presence of idealism has the potential to never leave and to ruin generations if not severed?

It is extremely important that ideals and all other soul ties are severed so that the cycles of repercussions rooted in the acts of the flesh are destroyed. This goes for any other ideal that you can think of. If you have an ideology that money can make you happy and solve all of your problems, you will be soul tied to money. If you have an ideology that the world's success will provide purpose and fulfillment to your life, you will be soul tied to the world's way and will die trying to achieve the next level or the next thing by the world's standards. Just as stifling, we have made the ideal of marriage and/or having a family the marker of fulfillment for our lives when another human being can never achieve that for us. The only way for complete fulfillment is through Jesus Christ, period. Everything else is temporary.

*An Appointed Time*

Ideologies are directly related to time. We often create ideologies that were never intended for our lives because we want to negate the time factor. We want to make something happen that was never intended at all or only intended for a specific period in our lives.

Every person that was on assignment in the Bible was given a specific assignment at an appointed time by God. The instructions were clear, given in God's timing, and an action was expected thereafter. Even now, if we negate any of these steps and become soul tied to our own timing and ideologies, we become immersed in disordered thinking and are being led by our flesh instead of the Holy Spirit. Thus, it is important that every ideology is rooted in God and God alone and that we always appreciate His appointed time for any instruction.

Godly ideologies are described below and are examples of living for God and being bound to His instruction at His appointed time.

*By faith Noah, when **warned** about things not yet seen, in holy fear built an ark to save his family. By his faith he condemned the world and became heir of the righteousness that is in keeping with faith. By faith Abraham, when **called** to go to a place he would later receive as his inheritance, obeyed and went, even though he did not know where he was going. By faith he made his home in the promised land like a stranger in a foreign country; he lived in tents, as did Isaac and Jacob, who were heirs with him of the same promise. For he was looking forward to the city with foundations, whose architect and builder is God. And by faith even Sarah, who was past childbearing age, was enabled to bear children because she*

*considered him faithful who had made the promise. And so from this one man, and he as good as dead, came descendants as numerous as the stars in the sky and as countless as the sand on the seashore.*
*-Hebrews 11:7-12*

The bolded words show the commands by God. Those commands were activated by faith and were then accompanied by action. This a Godly ideology, a conviction that comes directly from God. Their actions produced great spiritual fruit that we still feast from today. Had they operated in the flesh, none of the spiritual fulfillment in the Body of Christ would have ever come to pass. There would be no "us" had they operated in the flesh instead of the Spirit of God.

## Exhortation

I pray that discussing and reflecting on soul ties to ideals helps us to see the vile way the enemy uses our thoughts to create what we may perceive as "the way" when it's really his way leading to complete destruction of our lives. I pray that you walk in the way in the teaching of Peter.

*"Be alert and of sober mind. Your enemy the devil prowls around like a roaring lion looking for someone to devour. Resist him, standing firm in the faith, because you know that the family of believers throughout the world is undergoing the same kind of sufferings." -1 Peter 5:8-9*

## Chapter 9: Tasks, Roles, and Positions

Our everyday positions or roles and their associated tasks can either support our purpose or distract us from it. We have to be careful to identify when our souls and innate desires are tied to our roles or positions in life versus when they are tied the One who has ordained them. When we are participating in our roles, positions, or tasks and are consumed by them to the level that they become our god, our souls can create a bond that is an ungodly soul tie. When we are bonded to a position or task that is ordained by God and are performing it in the right constructs as instructed by God, we are involved in a Godly soul tie.

We must be very careful while operating in our God-appointed roles, tasks, or positions because it's easy to take a purposeful opportunity and pervert it into something that is idealistic, easily entangling ourselves in motives led by the acts of the flesh. We can all easily get caught up in "doing something for God" when, really, our motives become perverted and we seek our own gain (self-ambition) over truly seeking and serving the Kingdom of God. The latter is a Godly soul tie to tasks, roles, or positions, whereas the other is an ungodly soul tie.

In tying each soul tie concept together, our underlying motivations to each soul tie type directly intertwine and involve the others. For example, our soul ties to our roles, positions, and tasks intertwine with our soul ties to people, material possessions, and ideals. They all either support our operation within our purposes here on this earth or cause a complete waste of time if we are not careful and aware.

A beautiful reflection on where our hearts and minds should be in relation to God-given tasks, roles, or positions can be found in 1 Thessalonians. Paul writes to the church in Thessalonica regarding their faithfulness to the tasks, roles, and purpose at hand. The people were tied to the work that God had called them to because their motives were tied to God, who instructed them to do the work. This is reminiscent of the expectations God has for us to be tied to His Will and not at all tied to the world's motives of flaunting position and finding worth in status.

Paul initiates his appreciation of the Church:

*"We always thank God for all of you and continually mention you in our prayers. We remember before our God and Father **your work produced by faith, your labor prompted by love,** and your endurance inspired by hope in our Lord Jesus Christ."*
*-1 Thessalonians 1:2-3*

I love these Scriptures because they show the pure-hearted motives behind the work from the people of Thessalonica. It shows how our daily work (tasks, roles, or positions) should be unto the Lord. Our souls should be tied to the very intent of the Lord, not our own.

> *"For the appeal we make does not spring from error or impure motives, nor are we trying to trick you. On the contrary, we speak as those approved by God to be entrusted with the gospel. We are not trying to please people but God, who tests our hearts. You know we never used flattery, nor did we put on a mask to cover up greed - God is our witness. We were not looking for praise from people, not from you or anyone else, even though as apostles of Christ we could have asserted our authority. Instead, we were like young children among you." -1 Thessalonians 2:3-7*

What a power-packed Scripture! Let's unpack this and see how the Scriptures clearly say to be soul tied to God's purpose for our lives instead of succumbing to the world's direction.

"The appeal we make does not spring from error or impure motives": Their service, tasks, positions, and roles were intentional and unto God. There was no mistake or confusion behind what they did. They were pure at heart and free from impurity (an act of the flesh).

"Nor are we trying to trick you": They were free from witchcraft, discord, jealousy, selfish ambition, dissensions, and factions. There was no deceit present in their roles or positions when performing their God-given tasks.

"Those approved by God": Their call was approved by God. Paul was appreciative of them because their obedience produced spiritual fruit in his life and the lives of many others, therefore edifying the Kingdom of God.

"Entrusted with the gospel": This is the role, position, and task that God has called our souls to be tied to on this earth. In whatever roles God calls us to, He entrusts us to share the Gospel with not only our words but also our actions.

"We are not trying to please people but God": We are bound to God's Will, never to His people.

"We never used flattery, nor did we put on a mask to cover up greed": Being soul tied to God's Will for your life is created by faith and is filled with the fruit of the Spirit. It is holy and of God. You don't have to use manipulation or be led by the acts of the flesh, such as witchcraft, selfish ambition, or envy.

"We were not looking for praise from people, not from you or anyone else": We, as believers, are not on this earth to fulfill the desires or opinions of others. Our roles, positions, and tasks should be delegated by God. We should be looking for His approval, not man's.

"Even though as apostles of Christ we could have asserted our authority": No matter how superior we are considered by society, we are but dirt wrapped in filthy rags to God. Even though as apostles of Christ we could have asserted our authority, our said superiority does not trump God.

Our humility and obedience is our reasonable service to Him.

"Instead, we were like young children among you": References to children in the Bible reflect a submissive nature to God. Children are to be humble and submitted, awaiting their Father's instruction for what He has called them to do.

This breakdown of the Scriptures is meant to bring context to where our hearts and souls should be in our daily roles and tasks. It should be within the Will of God. Unfortunately, society has influenced our roles and associated tasks to become those that are outside of God's Will or purpose for our lives. We might be on a job or in a career that we've never been tasked to by God. We might be using a gift from God in our daily roles or positions in the wrong context; for example, using artistic talents in music or film in a way that breeds more confusion for the world and gratifies the flesh instead of the Spirit. You may be singing about sex and money, supporting the enemy's desire to keep you separated from the love of God. Or, you could be in a position or role that is considered to be "too good to be true" and that people would 'kill for," but you know that you're not supposed to be there. The benefits that keep you there are "too good" to leave. These are all ungodly soul ties to roles, positions, and tasks.

*"Do not deceive yourselves. If any of you think you are wise by the standards of this age, you should become 'fools' so that you may become wise. For the wisdom of this world is foolishness in God's sight." -1 Corinthians 3:18-19*

Anything outside of the Will of God for your life **will** eventually fall. It's inevitable. If God has been calling you, which I believe He has or you would have never picked up this book and started reading, He will only allow you to submit to the flesh for so long before He physically, mentally, and spiritually starts to dismantle your flesh. I'm speaking from experience!

Ungodly soul ties to roles or positions will have you in a pit of purposelessness and disobedience. Sometimes we think that if we are not doing what the world deems as successful then we won't be happy. It's the exact opposite; as long as we depend on the world to direct our emotions, we will never come to the fullness of our lives, which is obedience and joy. Ungodly soul ties may bring temporary happiness, but it is only that, temporary. The disobedience that comes along with it continues to invite the fruit of the flesh, which leads to death. Yes, it's that serious. Review the acts of the flesh you've seen displayed in real life, film, etc. Don't they always lead to death?

*"Nevertheless, each person should live as a believer in whatever situation the Lord has assigned to them, just as God has called them." -1 Corinthians 7:17*

So, what ungodly soul tie is God asking you to sever? What task(s) do you embark on daily that God has been calling you out of? There is no room for the excuse, "I have no other choice" or "What else would I do?" If you know you're not supposed to be doing it and you're still doing it, you're in disobedience. I'd rather you to stop now before the Lord initiates His jealousy followed by wrath. By severing an ungodly soul tie to a role or task you're not supposed to be in, He can then help you to have your full, undivided attention on Him and prepare you for your real purpose. Don't doubt God.

*"Therefore, my dear brothers and sisters, stand firm. Let nothing move you. Always give yourselves fully to the work of the Lord, because you know that your labor in the Lord is not in vain."*
*-1 Corinthians 15:58*

I've heard the phrase often, "His Will, His bill." Although it is catchy, it is also very true. If you're worried about not having financial stability, losing notoriety, or losing acceptance, God's presence and favor upon your life from obedience will always trump anything you've lost. In addition, His peace that surpasses all understanding will fulfill anything that you were trying to fulfill through the flesh in the first place. Nothing that is for or is done unto Him is in vain. He uses everything.

*"Do not be deceived: God cannot be mocked. A man reaps what He sows. Whoever sows to please their flesh, from the flesh will reap destruction; whoever sows to please the Spirit, from the Spirit will reap eternal life. Let us not become weary in doing good, for at the proper time we will reap a harvest if we do not give up. Therefore, as we have opportunity, let us do good to all people, especially to those who belong to the family of believers." -Galatians 6:7-10*

Your obedience in severing ungodly soul ties to tasks, positions, or roles is not just for your purpose, but it is also for the glory of God to be revealed to others. It is to edify the Kingdom of God when you are in His position. When you've learned to empty yourself from the acts of the flesh, you will be able to bless others because the fruit of the Spirit can feed the spirit of others through your obedience.

Pray for God's peace and righteous obedience upon your life right now. Let go of all God is instructing you to, particularly with ungodly soul ties to tasks, roles, or positions. I guarantee you that obedience is greater than sacrifice.

*"The Lord bless you and keep you; the Lord make His face shine on you and be gracious to you; the Lord turn his face toward you and give you peace." -Numbers 6:24-26*

## Chapter 10: Material Possessions

Soul ties to material possessions is undoubtedly one of the major demonic tactics in today's world. The enemy has such a veil and dominion in the spiritual realm. He uses motives of acquiring material possessions to keep souls tied to the acts of the flesh. I know of individuals who've attempted to sell their souls to the devil so that they could be forever tied to and accrue ownership to all the world's possessions. Well, the bad news for these individuals is that the enemy, in return, can only sell you a dream, a temporary vacation (this life), with all its potential possessions. In actuality, he is setting you up for eternal damnation in hell (which will go on forever) if you continue to allow your soul to be tied to physical idols.

If your soul is tied to material possessions, it is probably consequently involved with envy, greed, dissensions, factions, witchcraft, and idolatry. Think of those who have addictions to substances; access to one usually leads to another in order to gain a higher high. This is the same type of drive that happens for material possessions. What once seemed like a little envy or jealousy turns into dissensions and factions, ultimately to manipulate, steal, kill, and destroy (becomes idolatry and witchcraft). These are acts completely influenced by Satan and performed by the flesh. To sever the soul ties to material possessions is to understand the frailty in it and realize eternal treasure with God is the only thing worth possessing. It is perfectly okay to acquire possessions in a lifetime, but when they exceed in importance and honor over God, it is idolatry.

This is exactly what happened with King Solomon. He was the most powerful king in the Bible, due to his acquired wisdom from God, but he was largely known for his wealth (material possessions) and extravagant taste.

*"King Solomon was greater in riches and wisdom than all the other kings of the earth."*
*-1 Kings 10:23*

*"The weight of the gold that Solomon received yearly was 666 talents, not including the revenues from merchants and traders and from all the Arabian kings and the governors of the territories."*
*-1 Kings 10:14-15*

*"The king had a fleet of trading ships at sea along with the ships of Hiram. Once every three years it returned, carrying gold, silver and ivory, and apes and baboons."* *-1 Kings 10:22*

*"The whole world sought audience with Solomon to hear the wisdom God had put in his heart. Year after year, everyone who*

*came brought a gift - articles of silver and gold, robes, weapons and spices, and horses and mules." -1 Kings 10:24-25*

*"Solomon's daily provisions were thirty cors of the finest flour and sixty cors of meal, ten head of stall-fed cattle, twenty of pasture-fed cattle and a hundred sheep and goats, as well as deer, gazelles, roebucks and choice fowl. For he ruled over all the kingdoms west of the Euphrates River, from Tiphsah to Gaza, and had peace on all sides… Solomon had four thousand stalls for chariot horses, and twelve thousand horses." -1 Kings 4:22-24, 26*

*"God gave Solomon wisdom and very great insight, and a breadth of understanding as measureless as the sand on the seashore. Solomon's wisdom was greater than the wisdom of all the people of the East, and greater than all the wisdom of Egypt.*
*-1 Kings 4:29-30*

In this world, most people become tied to the idea of success or greatness through the possessions they attain. Clearly stated in Scripture, Solomon had every material possession imaginable, but he was only truly great because God had given him wisdom. Solomon's power came from God and God alone. He is the source to any greatness or success in this life. Our souls must be tied to Him and never to possessions.

*"At Gibeon the Lord appeared to Solomon during the night in a dream, and God said, 'Ask for whatever you want me to give you.' Solomon answered, 'You have shown great kindness to your servant, my father David, because he was faithful to you and righteous and upright in heart. You have continued this great kindness to him and have given him a son to sit on his throne this very day. Now, Lord my God, you have made your servant king in*

*place of my father David. But **I am only a little child and do
not know how to carry out my duties.** Your servant is here
among the people you have chosen, a great people, too numerous to
count or number. **So give your servant a discerning heart to
govern your people and to distinguish between right and
wrong.** For who is able to govern this great people of yours?' **The
Lord was pleased that Solomon had asked for this.** So God
said to him, '**Since you have asked for this and not for long
life or wealth for yourself, nor have asked for death of your
enemies but for discernment in administering justice, I will
do what you have asked. I will give you a wise and
discerning heart, so that there will never have been anyone
like you, nor will there ever be. Moreover, I will give you
what you have not asked for - both wealth and honor - so
that in your lifetime you will have no equal among kings.**
And if you walk in obedience to me and keep my decrees and
commands as David your father did, I will give you a long life.'
Then Solomon awoke - and he realized it had been a dream.*"
*-1 Kings 3:5-15*

King Solomon, as great as his lineage was already, still
knew to acknowledge God as his Source. In child-like
humility (because God is our heavenly Father), Solomon
went to God with a Kingdom-seeking mindset. He desired
for God to give him the ability to govern the people who
had been given to him with wisdom and discernment.
Solomon was concerned with and tied to the things of
God, His people, and God honored that. Because Solomon
came to God with pure motives, God rewarded him with
wealth, honor, and a long life. Solomon's riches were not
his priority or motive. He did not come to God to aid the
acts of the flesh but to grow the fruit of the Spirit. His
soul was tied to God's Will.

After God's decree to Solomon, he obeyed God and built the temple tasked to him. It took seven years to complete. God gave specific instructions to Solomon in creating the temple, and Solomon followed up with his extravagant taste and attention to detail. After building God's temple, Solomon built his own palace, which took thirteen years. Again, Solomon had all the material possessions he needed and ever wanted. Even with these possessions, God had His hand on Solomon and covered him.

*"When Solomon had finished building the temple of the Lord and the royal palace, and had achieved all he had desired to do, the Lord appeared to him a second time, as He had appeared to him at Gibeon. The Lord said to him: 'I have heard the prayer and plea you have made before me; I have consecrated this temple, which you have built, by putting my Name there forever. My eyes and my heart will always be there. As for you, if you walk before me faithfully with integrity of heart and uprightness, as David your father did, and do all I command and observe my decrees and laws, I will establish your royal throne over Israel forever, as I promised David your father when I said, 'You shall never fail to have a successor on the throne of Israel. But if you or your descendants turn away from me and do not observe the commands and decrees I have given you and go off to serve other gods and worship them, then I will cut off Israel from the land I have given them and will reject this temple I have consecrated for my Name.'"*
*-1 Kings 9:1-7*

Unfortunately, Solomon ended up submitting to the acts of the flesh instead of growing in the fruit of the Spirit. His soul became tied to the world, likely due to influences from his wealth.

*"King Solomon, however, loved many foreign women besides Pharaoh's daughter - Moabites, Ammonites, Edomites, Sidonians, and Hittites. They were from nations about which the Lord had told the Israelites, 'You must not intermarry with them, because they will surely turn your hearts after their gods.' Nevertheless, Solomon held fast to them in love. He had seven hundred wives of royal birth and three hundred concubines, and his wives led him astray. As Solomon grew old, his wives turned his heart after other gods, and his heart was not fully devoted to the Lord his God, as the heart of David his father had been... So Solomon did evil in the eyes of the Lord; he did not follow the Lord completely, as David his father had done." -1 Kings 11:1-4,6*

*"The Lord became angry with Solomon because his heart had turned away from the Lord, the God of Israel, who had appeared to him twice. Although he had forbidden Solomon to follow other gods, Solomon did not keep the Lord's command."*
*-1 Kings 11:9-10*

From Solomon's actions, the Lord promised him that He would tear the kingdom of Israel away from his lineage through his son, with the exception of one tribe. Solomon was the wealthiest of every king ever documented in the Bible, a gift given by God because of Solomon's initial position of obedience and pure heart. Because he later submitted to the acts of the flesh (greed, debauchery, impurity, sexual immorality, witchcraft, and idolatry), God separated himself from Solomon. Solomon defiled his promise to God.

Solomon was probably still the wealthiest in all the land after he repeatedly disobeyed God, but his riches were not great enough to sway God's Will for his life. God's desire was for Solomon to be obedient to Him. Solomon's riches could not buy God's acceptance, affection, or affirmation for his intentional sin. These actions were accepted by those in the kingdom of Israel, including his many wives and concubines, but God is not man. He is the Creator, not the creation.

Solomon literally had more than imaginable, but wealth and material possessions can never buy a heart position of obedience. Possessions can never enforce or create the presence of the fruit of the Spirit in someone's life. Material possessions are earthly, whereas the fruit of the Spirit continues on to heaven.

There are millionaires who worship their many possessions but have no love, joy, peace, forbearance, kindness, goodness, faithfulness, gentleness, or self-control. Those who put possessions above God often have no peace and go as far as taking their own lives. Only God can fill the missing portion that money can't buy. Homes, vehicles, property, clothing, money, and other investments/assets will all burn up before the judgment seat. They will never contribute to our treasury in heaven.

The Bible states, *"For where your treasure is, there your heart will be also" (Matthew 6:21)*. Thus, if your worth is determined by the material items you possess; or more directly stated, if your soul is tied to them, that's where your heart will be, and you will be judged for it. God doesn't judge your belongings or acquirements, He judges your heart. What does your heart speak? Where does your soul lie? God knows if your soul is attached to possessions easier than any man could ever judge. If your soul desires a certain lifestyle and you "use God" to get it, He knows that too. What owns you and who you belong to (God or Satan) will be ever so clear.

Our souls will be passed through the fire. Anything unlike God will be burned in the flames. So, again, where does your soul lie?

*"I have learned the secret of being content in any and every situation, whether well fed or hungry, whether living in plenty or in want." -Philippians 4:12*

We must have the revelation that in whatever we think we want or desire, God has already supplied all of our **needs**. Everything additional is surplus, and all will burn up in the fire before the judgment seat (Revelation 20:11). Everything we need is already in the storehouse. This means God has already provided the things that we need and made it all freely available to us. This goes beyond things or material possessions. It is evident in what is freely given through the fruit of the Spirit.

*"And my God will meet all your needs according to the riches of his glory in Christ Jesus."*
*-Philippians 4:19*

So, whether we have plenty or are in want, and whether we have little or surplus like King Solomon, God calls our hearts to be tied to His Will. Possessions are of benefit in this earth for the appropriate reasons and times. They were never intended to be idols or excuses for disobedience to what God has called for us to do. If anything, they are to be used as blessings to help others.

I pray that every reader will no longer be tied to things that will one day burn up with this world. Our main concern should be where our soul will be one day, with God or Satan. We cannot allow the entitlement that comes along with society's view of having material possessions deter us from eternal concern and obedience. Let's refocus our minds back on the Will of God, no matter what we do or do not have.

# THE SEVERING PROCESS

## Chapter 11: What Feeds Our Soul Ties?

*"You cannot drink the cup of the Lord and the cup of demons too;
you cannot have a part in both the Lord's table and the table of
demons. Are we trying to arouse the Lord's jealousy? Are we
stronger than He?" -1 Corinthians 10:21-22*

We cannot continue to say that we want to sever our soul
ties when we continue to partake in those things that link
us directly to them. If so, the Scripture tells us directly
that we are being disobedient, arousing the Lord's
jealousy. Based on this Scripture's description of
disobedience and entertaining the enemy's advances,
doing so exhibits defiance and is seen as "challenging"
God; hence it saying, *"Are we stronger than He?"* Of course
not. Only God can restore us from severing every soul tie
we've ever been exposed to. Unfortunately, when we
continue to drink from the cup of demons (be fed by the
enemy), we continue to engross ourselves in the fruit of

the flesh, creating further soul ties. So, in order to start and maintain the severing process, we must identify what feeds our soul ties.

With the hope of identifying some contributing factors to engaging in ungodly soul ties, I'd like to explore a few actions that have been issues in my own life. I pray that it will bring awareness of limitations in your life.

### Reminiscing Thoughts

How often does reminiscing about sin genuinely put a smile on our faces? We quickly forget about the matrix of sin and soul ties that engulfed us and the years that is has taken to recover from it. We may think about the fast money we used to make but forget about the legal trouble that it entangled us in (greed). We may bask in how we used to use profane language and argue with anyone just to have the last word (dissension and factions). We may reminisce on what we used to have: the cars, clothes, trips, and other luxuries that came with being tied to or manipulated by a person or situation (idolatry and witchcraft). And last but not least, we may constantly reminisce on the "what ifs" from the relationships that God never told us to engage in or has told us to break away from (impurity).

What benefit is it to our soul and its deliverance and restoration to continue to engage in reminiscing thoughts and conversation? The enemy loves a playground, and that's exactly what happens when we reminisce about our past. When these thoughts start to manifest, the Holy

Spirit has given us the power to shut them down! The Word states that He will give us a way out (1 Corinthians 10:13). His way out in this matter is to take control of our thoughts and shut them off. The Lord did not give us a spirit of fear, but of power, love, and a sound mind (2 Timothy 1:7). If He has given us a sound mind, then we must tap into it and tell our thoughts who they belong to. They belong to God, not to the devil and his corruptive lies.

### Excuses

We must be beyond using excuses such as, "We have history," "This is just who I am," "There's nothing wrong with doing this and serving God," "The Lord knows my heart," and "He is still working on me." When we say these phrases, it's a legitimate slap in the face to God. It's almost as if we're saying that sending His Son to this earth to die for our ways, soul ties, and shortcomings wasn't enough, and that the power through His Son is not strong enough to overcome whatever we're making excuses about.

If your soul is legitimately tied to something, a person, etc., and God is begging you to be free of it, stop making excuses. Surrender. God is waiting on you.

### Music

This subject is the most difficult for me to write about. Music is one of my absolute favorite enjoyments. I love all genres, and it genuinely influences my creativity. Yet, as my relationship with God has become more deep and sincere, He has explicitly narrowed down the musical selection that He allows me to listen to.

For one main reason, music is like a time machine. It can take you back to a specific moment in time with one musical chord, eventually making up an assimilation of sounds and memories. That one song will have you right back in a matrix of soul ties, to any moment in any act of the flesh. As stated earlier, God is a jealous God. He does not desire for us to use music or anything else to stay bonded to ungodly soul ties. Thus, relating music to the reminiscing thoughts, you can listen to one song and get emotionally back in the bed with the person God is trying to deliver you from. You can be back in whatever manipulative (witchcraft) and idolatrous situation that you've been seeking to be free from for years.

Deliverance can be dismantled with one song. The enemy knows music better than anyone because he was once a purveyor of it in heaven. He knows exactly how to use it to get us off course and to deny God. We must seek God and ask for direction in everything that we take in through the ear, eye, and mouth gates.

Also, think about how music can put us in a trance and allow us to escape from our realities. We have to be very careful of our motives for engaging in musical composition. If we are not careful, the very words or compositions we are listening to will have us reconnecting or creating a new soul tie. Yes, it goes that deep.

I am using music as an example because it is the main media source that feeds my soul ties. Yet, the same explanations can apply to TV, all forms of social media, or any other forms of media that feed your desire to sin.

### Consistently Exposing Yourself to the Soul Tie

Whatever soul tie you are seeking deliverance from, you must first stop exposing yourself to it. Stop engaging in it. Stop submitting yourself to it. Your exposure to it is keeping you bound. Stop answering the texts and calls or engaging in interactions from men or women God has instructed you to sever from your life. Stop allowing the fast money to control you and keep you bound to sin. Stop allowing your family member's behavior and your interactions from past experiences with them control the decision making for your life.

I'm suggesting that you stop *all* communication and interactions with any links to your former soul ties, even if it comes with having to move, quit a job, or discontinue communication with a loved one for a time period. You have to do what you have to do. Your soul needs to be bonded to only One. There is no room for void fillers and idols. Again, separating from the exposure to these soul ties does not mean to "run away" from the issues; but you must follow the leading of the Holy Spirit, the peace that resounds in your heart, to separate yourself from any connection to the soul tie.

*Exhortation*

Brothers and sisters, learn to take heed, using the wisdom and knowledge God has given you to no longer feed these soul ties. There is someone out there awaiting your obedience to clearly hear from the Lord and do what He has called you to do so that you can eventually help them.

*"Finally, brothers and sisters, whatever is true, whatever is noble, whatever is right, whatever is pure, whatever is lovely, whatever is admirable - if anything is excellent or praiseworthy - think about such things." -Philippians 4:8*

## Chapter 12:  How to Cut Off a Soul Tie

The process of cutting off or severing a soul tie can vary depending on the circumstance. How you cut off an ungodly soul tie from a family member will differ from how you cut of a soul tie from an ungodly romantic relationship. Those scenarios will also differ from cutting off soul ties to greed or poor financial management. Although we've touched on this process in each chapter, I want to take time to discuss and review some basic steps to severing soul ties. In addition, I'd like to address a few more topics that plague Western society and often are not associated or explained as soul ties.

_Step 1: Stop Running from God_
If He's been speaking to you, pushing you to make the right decision that He's explicitly told you to, stop running! You are unnecessarily prolonging your torment and disabling your purpose. The crying, the sadness, the

grief, the disbelief, and the pain can all stop if you just say, "Yes, God." Just tell Him, "Yes!" You are wasting time. There's someone out there waiting on your obedience, waiting on you to disband this soul tie that you know is present in your life. Stop running!

### Step 2: Acknowledge the Soul Tie and Pray Over It
Do you realize that our most powerful weapon is intercession in the spirit realm that allows us to petition God and cut off the devil? When we belong to God, we have the authority and power to call out our flesh (sin) and seek deliverance and wholeness through Christ. This means no more soul ties. Through prayer, we petition heaven to come down here on earth. (This is what the prayer portion *"as it is in heaven"* refers to.) We can pray for God's perfect Will over our lives instead of sin. This can only take effect once we acknowledge there is a soul tie that we actually need to petition God for.

### Step 3: Get Quiet
Some will think of this step solely as praying about your soul tie and getting quiet before the Lord so He can teach you how to handle it. Yes, that's a part of it, but it is not all of it. I love the Scripture that says, *"And we know that in all things God works for the good of those who love Him, who have been called according to His purpose"* (Romans 8:28). So in God's sovereign and infinite wisdom, we can rejoice that our circumstances, even our soul ties, will benefit and honor God if we stay along for His process in working through them. This goes beyond a daily quiet time; this is an expectation of God's glory to be revealed even in our most nasty situations. Get quiet means to rest and wait for His glory to be revealed in the circumstances. I never

knew my "Get Quiet" portion would take several years and eventually birth a book. Yahweh!

### Step 4: Choose Deliverance

Deliverance is the choice to reject sin and intentionally choose righteousness. We can all say that we have severed our soul ties, but do our heart positions and actions demonstrate that daily? Do we state that we are delivered when we're really still struggling, going through the motions of resisting the sin, and actually failing? Again, we have power in our words and actions. With Jesus Christ being our true Lord and Savior, we rely on Him to powerfully overcome anything of the flesh because His sacrifice covered all struggles leading to soul ties. We have the power through Jesus Christ to continuously choose deliverance, be marked with true change, and turn away from every single thing that once so easily entangled (Hebrews 12:1).

### Step 5: Cut Off the Residuals

Cutting off a soul tie does not just mean declaring over, praying about, and exiting the issue from your life. It also means that those actions need to be applied to everything that fed and was produced from the soul tie. So, in the case of financial soul ties, don't frequent the places that you know you have poor control in, such as your favorite store. Don't think about calling the bank to reopen the credit card account that God has explicitly told you to close. Stop replaying the enemy's lies that have said you will always be in debt just like your parents.

For the ungodly relationship, stop answering the calls and texts, period! Stop trying to justify spending time with someone God has told you to not have any interaction with just because you're bored. Stop feeding your bondage to people by continuing to compare yourself to those on social media. Take out everything in your home that reminds you of that soul tie. Cut off all interactions with any people that lead you down the wrong path, no matter the costs. Get a new number, stop frequenting the place you know they're at, and stop reaffirming negativity within your life to feed the insecurities. Sever every residual thing that feeds your soul ties! Exude self-control.

### Step 6: Consecrate Yourself

In order for any of the aforementioned steps to be long lasting and effective, you must consecrate yourself regularly. This is what Paul speaks of in Romans 12:1-2. *"Therefore, I urge you, brothers and sisters, in view of God's mercy, to offer your bodies as a living sacrifice, holy and pleasing to God - this is your true and proper worship. Do not conform to the pattern of this world, but be transformed by the renewing of your mind. Then you will be able to test and approve what God's Will is - His good, pleasing and perfect Will."*

Consecration is the act of offering ourselves solely and purely to God. This includes our soul, thoughts, and actions. Consecration can be sought through the twelve spiritual disciplines. I encourage you to research and enact these disciplines so that you can continue in and strengthen your deliverance process of severing soul ties. The twelve spiritual disciplines are: prayer, fasting, meditation, study, simplicity, submission, solitude, service, confession, guidance, celebration, and worship. Consecration is a daily process, like deliverance. It is a constant sacrifice we make to get closer to God through the disciplining of our flesh.

Following these steps is not an immediate formula or a comprehensive list for severing soul ties. God is the ultimate resource, and He will guide you from the foundation of these points into every detail of your individual process. The key to overcoming anything in the flesh is keeping your eyes on Him consistently. The good news is that everything in the flesh has already been overcome through the Blood of Jesus Christ.

### *For Those Who Have Suffered from Various Forms of Abuse*

I understand that there could have been chapter upon chapter written specifically about this subject. Much like family soul ties, abuse runs extremely deep. I pray that the chapters that have come before this, addressing other forms of soul ties, have helped to identify and start the severing process for the origins of abuse experiences. The soul ties addressed prior can be foundational to or contributing factors in abuse experiences.

There are a number of men and women who have suffered from physical, mental, emotional, and sexual abuse that has rocked them to their core. (In childhood, particularly, this happens more than we think or realize.) Consequences of this include difficulty in submitting to authority or the inability to commit to any type of relationship (associations, friendships, or romantic relationships) because of a fear of vulnerability. Coping mechanisms include jumping from relationship to relationship, attempting to gratify completion and healing. The sexually abused may inadvertently find themselves with many sexual partners, and the physically or mentally abused may adversely engage in relationships with physical or mental abuse. This revolving door causes a continuation of bondage for the abused. This solves nothing. The initial sinful exposure in the abused causes cyclical effects that can continue for a lifetime.

To severe soul ties of abuse, first utilize the list above as a foundation. Secondly, rely on the Holy Spirit to provide wisdom for the right resources to assist you and to even walk alongside you in your healing and restoration. Thirdly, pray for direction in seeking additional services, such as Christian counseling networks or true accountability. Accountability partners can be other Christian men or women (gender specific suggested) who have gone through similar experiences.

No one is defined by the abuse that they've endured. The most frequently asked question is, "Why would God allow the abuse to happen to me?" It is a very difficult question to answer. The best way is by recalling the abuse that Jesus endured, both emotional and physical, on the cross. God knew it was happening and was still with Jesus through it all. The good news is that all souls were saved from it! Just like Jesus, we have to believe that our experiences, even the abuse that our souls have been tied to, can produce a saving harvest in our lives and for the lives of others. Of course, no one should ever have to go through any form of abuse. But, if God allowed it, there is a far greater purpose behind it. Jesus Christ has given us direct access to be severed from every soul tie, separated and forgiven from all sin forevermore. Sin was covered and atoned for when Jesus died and arose from the dead. This includes the abuse (sin) that was performed to you, as well as the guilt and shame that you've carried thereafter.

*"'He himself bore our sins' in His body on the cross, so that we might die to sins and live for righteousness; 'by His wounds you have been healed.'" -1 Peter 2:24*

God has given us the power to no longer be bound by any sin experience through the Blood of Jesus Christ. Because of this, our experiences don't define us and can be used to save and encourage deliverance for someone else! In spite of our feelings and a probable constant desire to submit to our flesh from the hurt and pain, I pray we will keep our eyes on the sovereign, infinite, and great God that we serve for healing and wholeness in severing all soul ties from abuse.

### Soul Ties Developed Within Relationships That Now Involve Children

This is another very sensitive and real subject. I've seen the effects and consequences of soul ties between parents who aren't married and the consequential soul tie effects of their children all too well.

As you know, this was the situation with my mother and father. In the past six or so years, I've been able to relate my desires of being submitted to ungodly soul ties to my parent's ungodly soul tie relationship. Not that it was ever their intention to have an ungodly soul tie relationship, but the truth of the matter is that sin definitely has generational consequences.

My mother chose to stay with my dad for almost thirty years before she recognized her soul tie and decided to begin the severing process. She probably didn't realize that there was a spiritual stronghold between their two souls that kept her bound for so long, and the same goes for him as well. Being in the midst of it all, my involvement in this bondage consequently created a need within my soul that mimicked their needs. Therefore, I believe this contributed to the initiation of my desires for ungodly soul ties. Do you see the generational consequences and why these types of relationships need to be severed?

Thus, if you are a woman or man who is continuing in a relationship with the father or mother of your child even though you know God has told you that you're unequally yoked, you are in an ungodly soul tie that needs to be severed. Furthermore, you are in disobedience to God. Just as I've spoken of my personal example, your child also could carry on this ungodly generational mindset and desire ungodly soul ties because of examples they've observed through you and the other parent. You must stop this generational proposition from the enemy now.

I understand that having a soul tie to someone you've had a child with is much more complicated than if the ungodly soul tie only involved the two individuals without the child. Yet, if God is calling you to sever the soul tie, you must do it. Your child's future obedience to God is at stake. Just think of how many of us are trying to recover from our childhoods because of the ungodly soul ties we've witnessed our parents being in bondage to.

Addressing the ungodly soul ties between unequally yoked parents is not a quest to break up a family structure for the child, but it is a quest to establish order between men and women (2 Corinthians 6:14). A person, man or woman, parent or not, won't be able to fruitfully act within God's Will for their lives, especially in raising a child, when they are out of order and being disobedient to God. This means you cannot effectively raise your child in the ammunition of the Lord when you have an ungodly soul tie looming, even when that tie is to their other parent. Obedience needs to be established between the two of you individually. Each of you must desire individual, holy relationships with God. A child should not be raised within an ungodly soul tie relationship. If they are, you are automatically setting them up for generational consequences of disobedience in their lives. I know because I've lived it. My consequential soul ties and generational mindset had to be severed.

### What Happens When You Feel Like You're Knee Deep and There's No Way Out of Your Soul Tie Situation?

*"And God is faithful; he will not let you be tempted beyond what you can bear. But when you are tempted, he will also provide a way out so that you can endure it." -1 Corinthians 10:13*

This is the answer to the question. God will give you a way out. You will be able to endure the circumstances because He will give you a path to take. It may not be easy, but it will be your custom-made path by God to sever your soul tie. You have to sincerely believe this. There is no situation too deep or difficult to get out of when God has cleared the way for you. There will be a process, but He can and will get you out of it if you just depend on and rest in Him. No matter what heartache has been established, no matter the contentions or history, God can and will get you out of (sever) the soul tie that has you so bound. There's no amount of money, history, or association that is bigger than God. Please allow Him to come into your heart and sever your soul ties. You have to believe that God is with you and that following His Will is always better than your current situation.

### Soul Ties to the Dead

This is a difficult subject to write about, but it is very real. We naturally have soul ties to loved ones, even after death. Yet, many people remain bound from living purposeful lives because of their bondage to the dead. We have overlooked that people bondage can last beyond death. Those involved in this type of ungodly soul tie feel like their lives don't have purpose without their loved one being present. These individuals may obsess over their loved one's life, accomplishments, anniversaries, birthday, etc.

It is healthy to mourn the loss and go through the stages of grief, but it is unhealthy to stay there. No one can be the judge of how long someone should mourn their loved one, but when it becomes an idol and a distraction in their lives, it is a form of people bondage. The deceased can begin to take precedence in someone's life above God. This is an ungodly soul tie.

Just as it was encouraged in the abuse section, I would advise someone dealing with significant grief that limits their participation and purpose in life to seek professional counseling and accountability. If a death is inhibiting their relationship with God and keeping them bound to the deceased, this is a very real, spiritual issue. Professional and spiritual advisement is suggested because it not only affects the person whose soul is tied but also their extended family, loved ones, and associates.

### Prayer to Sever Soul Ties

Lord, I know that the enemy is looming. I know that the enemy might be in the ear of each person who is reading this book at this very moment. Lord God, I ask for You to bind every tactic, lie, and story of deception that is trying to overcome the reader and make them think that the soul tie cannot be cut off. I pray that even the deepest of soul ties are severed in this very moment and that there is a complete release and relief within the soul of each reader.

I pray that we do not return to the bondage, but that we choose deliverance daily. I thank You that a relationship with You takes priority over any desire to be bound to ungodly ties to people, material possessions, ideals, or tasks. We bless Your Holy Name for deliverance. In Jesus' name we pray, amen.

# Chapter 13: Psalms

Is God petitioning you to cry out to Him, but you won't? Are you still attempting to endure that painful place in your life? The deeply-rooted issues are finally surfacing.

You thought you were over it, right? Why is it so hard to leave that toxic relationship? Has the worship of that relationship come to an end, and has God shown you how He is the only righteous One that can be eternally jealous for you?

Are perverse thoughts continuing to replay in your mind and keep you bound to the idea of something or someone?

Think about the words and actions that were expressed to you and told you that you were insignificant, not good enough, ugly, unworthy, or stupid; you have kept those words, thoughts, and actions with you until this day. They are deeply rooted and demonic, not allowing you to break free.

The alcohol, marijuana, cocaine, or prescription pills cause no solidarity or peace within your spirit. The substances have gotten you nowhere, and you want to finally be fully free, not just free in a period of sobriety.

Your parent's hurtful words or actions from childhood stop you from living purposefully in adulthood.

The title, position, and benefits have you enslaved and envious of others. Are you afraid that if you stop now and walk away from the fame or comfort that your soul is tied to, you will no longer have significance?

Time is your stressor: next week, month, or year.

The list and categories of worry, stress, unforgiveness, toxicity, and other forms of bondage could continue for the extent of this book. We have an opportunity to stop basking in the flesh and replace every issue with the Spirit of God. At this very moment, God is probably in full force, revealing some things to you that you are still holding on to. Let it go. Staying in that place pollutes your heart. These things are like spoiled milk or rotten food. They have just been sitting there, unfulfilled and without purpose. They are burdens and bondage. Bondage to people, tasks or positions, ideals, or material possessions rule your every moment and consume you. This bondage plagues you.

Years ago, I was introduced to the book of Psalms as letters or prayers to God. King David's hope in these writings was for God to meet and direct him through and beyond every iniquity, wrongdoing, frustration, insecurity, and any other sin he had committed. David was laying down every soul tie at the helm of the Lord.

The goal of this chapter is to encourage you to reflect, have some personal and quiet time with God, address the places where your heart has become polluted, and pour out every frustration and circumstance that has kept your soul tied for far too long. You know exactly what is holding you back from a righteous relationship with Jesus Christ. The most unfortunate thing is when people believe that laying their burdens down has to look pretty or that it happens all at once. In reality, this process might be accompanied by falling on the ground in distress, an ugly cry, blaming yourself, reflecting with the "what ifs," rationalizing the issues, and even considering that choosing Jesus is not worth it.

The enemy will certainly try to confuse you in the midst of your deliverance. There has to be a point in our lives where we realize that submitting to the enemy's lies does not work. It is worth it to seek the Savior who has already come to this earth to save and redeem us from every sin we've ever committed. So, like David in Psalms, submit every piece of mess, frustration, lack, insecurity, fear, stressor, worry, and impure moment to God right now.

I have listed some of my favorite Scriptures from the book of Psalms from a time I was at my lowest, my breaking point. Even as I've been faced with ridding myself of thoughts and actions to get closer to God, I find myself back in these Scriptures, crying out to God for His reassurance and basking in His love for me. Although these Scriptures were written before the New Testament's "fruit of the Spirit" Scriptures, they show how His love is eternal and absent from time. In Psalms, He showered His love on David before He sent His Son who eventually provided the Holy Spirit who now comforts us. This shows us that time is not a factor with God. His Word never returns void and always holds true.

So, read and repeat these Scriptures to yourself in affirmation, journal with meditation, or read them as prayers to God. However the Holy Spirit is leading you, rid yourself now of every pain, strife, and action that has kept you bound.

*"Answer me when I call to you, my righteous God. Give me relief from my distress; have mercy on me and hear my prayer."*
*-Psalm 4:1*

*"And the words of the Lord are flawless, like silver purified in a crucible, like gold refined seven times." -Psalm 12:6*

*"But I trust in your unfailing love; my heart rejoices in your salvation. I will sing the Lord's praise, for He has been good to me." -Psalm 13:5-6*

*"Lord, you alone are my portion and my cup; you make my lot secure."-Psalm 16:5*

*"May these words of my mouth and this meditation of my heart be pleasing in your sight, Lord, my Rock and my Redeemer."*

-Psalm 19:14

"Even though I walk through the darkest valley, I will fear no evil,
for you are with me; your rod and your staff, they comfort me."
-Psalm 23:4

"Show me your ways, Lord, teach me your paths. Guide me in your
truth and teach me, for you are God my Savior, and my hope is in
you all day long." -Psalm 25:4-5

"For his anger lasts only a moment, but his favor lasts a lifetime;
weeping may stay for the night, but rejoicing comes in the
morning." -Psalm 30:5

"I sought the Lord, and he answered me; he delivered me from all
my fears." -Psalm 34:4

"The angel of the Lord encamps around those who fear him, and he
delivers them."
-Psalm 34:7

"Taste and see that the Lord is good; blessed is the one who takes
refuge in Him. Fear the Lord, you his holy people, for those who
fear him lack nothing. The lions may grow weak and hungry, but
those who seek the Lord lack no good thing." -Psalm 34:8-10

"The righteous cry out, and the Lord hears them; he delivers them
from all their troubles."
-Psalm 34:17

**"The Lord is close to the brokenhearted and saves those
who are crushed in spirit."**
-Psalm 34:18

*"The righteous person may have many troubles, but the Lord delivers him from them all; He protects all his bones, not one of them will be broken."-Psalm 34:19-20*

*"Be still before the Lord and wait patiently for him; do not fret when people succeed in their ways, when they carry out their wicked schemes."-Psalm 37:7*

*"The Lord makes firm the steps of the one who delights in him; though he may stumble, he will not fall, for the Lord upholds him with his hand." -Psalm 37:23-24*

*"My sacrifice, O God, is a broken spirit; a broken and contrite heart you, God, will not despise."*
*-Psalm 51:17*

*"Save me, O God, by your name; vindicate me by your might. Hear my prayer, O God, listen to the words of my mouth."*
*-Psalm 54:1-2*

*"Surely God is my help; the Lord is the one who sustains me."*
*-Psalm 54:4*

*"Listen to my prayer, O God, do not ignore my plea; hear me and answer me. My thoughts trouble me and I am distraught."*
*-Psalm 55:1-2*

*"As for me, I call to God, and the Lord saves me. Evening, morning and noon I cry out in distress, and he hears my voice. He rescues me unharmed from the battle waged against me, even though many oppose me." -Psalm 55:16-18*

*"Cast your cares on the Lord and He will sustain you; he will never let the righteous be shaken."*
*-Psalm 55:22*

*"On my bed I remember you; I think of you through the watches of the night. Because you are my help, I sing in the shadow of Your wings. I cling to you; Your right hand upholds me."*
*-Psalm 63:6-8*

*"But as for me, it is good to be near God. I have made the Sovereign Lord my refuge; I will tell of all your deeds."* *-Psalm 73:28*

*"Praise the Lord, my soul; all my inmost being, praise His holy name. Praise the Lord, my soul, and forget not all his benefits - who forgives all your sins and heals all your diseases, who redeems your life from the pit and crowns you with love and compassion, who satisfies your desires with good things so that your youth is renewed like the eagle's."* *-Psalm 103:1-5*

*"Give thanks to the Lord, for he is good; his loves endures forever."*
*-Psalm 107:1*

*"Remember your word to your servant, for you have given me hope. My comfort in my suffering is this: Your promise preserves my life."*
*-Psalm 119:49-50*

*"I lift up my eyes to the mountains - where does my help come from? My help comes from the Lord, the Maker of heaven and earth. He will not let your foot slip - he who watches over you will not will not slumber."* *-Psalm 121:1-3*

*"The Lord will keep you from all harm - he will watch over your life; the Lord will watch over your coming and going both now and forevermore." -Psalm 121:7-8*

*"Unless the Lord builds the house, the builders labor in vain. Unless the Lord watches over the city, the guards stand watch in vain." -Psalm 127:1*

*"I praise you because I am fearfully and wonderfully made; Your works are wonderful, I know that full well." -Psalm 139:14*

*"He heals the brokenhearted and binds up their wounds." -Psalm 147:3*

## Chapter 14: Deliverance

So what's next after crying out? Do you stay in your despair? No! You become delivered from your ungodly soul ties by severing them! Deliverance, or severing your soul ties, happens when you identify your sin, seek God to transform your heart, and incur a heart change that is fed with the fruit of the Spirit (love, joy, peace, forbearance, kindness, goodness, faithfulness, gentleness and self-control).

The text of the often misused Scripture, *"He'll bring you the desires of your heart"* (Psalm 37:4), actually means that we are to align ourselves with His Word and truths. His desires will become our desires, including being set free from ungodly soul ties. God sending His Son, Jesus, was meant as a pure sacrifice for the deliverance of all sin, even from soul ties here on earth! That's why we need Jesus. His atoning sacrifice paid the price for every ungodly soul tie and gave us the power and authority to overcome its tempting presence in every situation. Deliverance is not in our own strength, ever. Jesus has provided the Way, the Truth, and the Life for us and our circumstances.

It cannot be reiterated enough. Deliverance happens with acknowledgement of the soul tie, a steadfast pursuit of God (through spiritual discipline), and a heart change to look like His. Deliverance happens when you hate the sin you once loved. You are completely uncomfortable with the thought of doing it again and the idea of going back is repulsive. Deliverance is obedience to God in spite of the intensity of the temptation to become bonded again to the previous soul tie.

By this point, maybe God has been beckoning at your heart. Maybe He has been petitioning you to surrender your entire life to Him, but you still haven't. Maybe He is calling you to holiness (being set apart) and righteousness (a byproduct of holiness), but you're still holding on to those unrighteous desires. Let's now take an in-depth look at the spiritual implications of our deliverance and the journey that is involved.

In Romans 1, God speaks through Paul about His wrath against sinful humanity.

*"The wrath of God is being revealed from heaven against all the godlessness and wickedness of people, **who suppress the truth by their wickedness**, since what may be known about God is plain to them, because God has made it plain to them. -Romans 1:18-19*

These Scriptures identity two things. One, they identify that we, in the flesh, can suppress the truth by our wickedness. The interesting thing about this is that although we choose to remain wicked, the truth can only be suppressed, **not** destroyed. God's Word always lives, even when we die.

Two, these Scriptures re-confirm what God revealed to me in this book's introduction. Our godlessness and wickedness has been made completely plain because God has revealed it to us individually. We actually know the power of God, but again, we choose to suppress His truth by our wickedness. This is extremely dangerous territory and stifles the opportunity for deliverance completely.

*For since the creation of the world God's invisible qualities - his eternal power and divine nature - have been clearly seen, being understood from what has been made, so that people are without excuse. -Romans 1:20*

Again, God plainly shows us who He is. He is the foundation. His eternal power and divine nature have been here since the beginning. We cannot deny His presence because it is seen wherever we go: in the trees, vast land, mountainous structures, deep oceans, and all the animals. We are without excuse that there is a God, One who has made all creations of this world. Just as these creations must bow down and obey the almighty God (through how they grow, shed, develop, etc. within each season), we, too, as a creation of the almighty God should bow down to His Will for our lives, one that is righteous and not unrighteous or self-righteous. We are without excuse.

To reiterate, when we remain disobedient and choose to continue our engagement of the flesh instead of choosing the Spirit, God will give us over to the depravities of our minds.

*For although they knew God, they neither glorified him as God nor gave thanks to him, but their thinking became futile and their foolish hearts were darkened. Although they claimed to be wise, they became fools and **exchanged the glory of the immortal God for images** made to look like a mortal human being and birds and animals and reptiles. -Romans 1:21-23*

This is our constant fight in our mortal bodies. The enemy wants us to exchange the glory of the immortal God for counterfeit. This is our struggle between the flesh and the Spirit. One is a counterfeit, a distraction, while the Spirit is the truth, our helper from God to lead us in holiness and righteousness.

Righteousness leads to productivity within our lives instead of death. The Word of God is plain to tell us that once we have been warned and continue to choose to live with futile and foolish hearts, we have now denied God's Holy Spirit and our hearts **will** be darkened.

So where does deliverance take place in all of humanity's mayhem? Immediately after God's description of His wrath, He discloses, *"... the riches of His kindness, forbearance and patience. God's kindness is intended to lead you to repentance"* (Romans 2:4).

Repentance is the complete turning away from sin. A repentant heart hates sin as God does. Thus, when we accept God and choose to live as He says, we are engulfed with His riches of kindness, forbearance, and patience.

144

**Deliverance is choosing God in every moment of our lives.** We have a daily choice to continue to choose counterfeits of the flesh, where the devil presents temptation after temptation for what appears to be good and beneficial when God has revealed that it is not. Or, we could choose righteousness through the Spirit that reaps great heavenly rewards. Choosing the Spirit creates freedom from the bondage of sin, thus inhabiting deliverance. Deliverance is a byproduct of freedom through righteousness. Deliverance encompasses the fullness of one's spirit when they choose God (the Spirit of God) over their flesh. This deliverance gives us the power to be freed from soul ties.

If we can only be delivered through righteousness, what is righteousness? *"For it is not those who hear the law who are righteous in God's sight, but it is those who obey the law who will be declared righteous"* (Romans 2:13). *"Therefore no one will be declared righteous in God's sight by the works of the law; rather, through the law we become conscious of our sin"* (Romans 3:20).

Thus, between these two passages, righteousness happens through the obedience and actions of God's Word. The actions of the Word of God are always more spiritual than physical because the spiritual actions guide all physical actions. Righteousness comes by obeying the Spirit of God in all facets of our lives. Yet, if it were this easy to just transform our flesh to inhabiting the Spirit of God, wouldn't we all be doing it? It takes a connection that goes beyond our flesh. Righteousness is given through **faith** in Christ Jesus to all who believe. God presented Christ as a sacrifice of atonement, through the shedding of his blood, to be received by faith. He did it to demonstrate

His righteousness at the present time and to justify those who have faith in Jesus (Romans 3:22, 25-26).

So, do you believe that Jesus Christ can provide righteousness through faith, creating a repentant heart reaping deliverance? I know He can because He's done it for me. I am praying that you will bask in His presence and allow Him to change you, soul tie by soul tie. He cares deeply for you and wants you delivered.

*"He has delivered us from such a deadly peril, and he will deliver us again. On him we have set our hope that he will continue to deliver us." -2 Corinthians 1:10*

# Chapter 15: Being Healed and Whole

Our bondage to ungodly soul ties has hindered us from true healing and wholeness in our lives. As believers, we know that being healed and whole only comes from the redemptive power of Jesus Christ, who was sent by God as an atoning sacrifice. We no longer depend on our own flesh, people, material possessions, roles or positions, tasks, or ideals to complete our lives on this earth. We rely on our relationship with God to create the appropriate details of our lives to bring Him glory and also to provide our completion as spiritual, emotional, and physical beings.

*"For we know that our old self was crucified with him so that the body ruled by sin might be done away with, that we should no longer be slaves to sin - because anyone who has died has been set free from sin." -Romans 6:6*

The difficulty we have in our complete deliverance is the desire to pick our sin back up. Our declaration, that Jesus Christ has conquered all sin, gives us the authority and power over anything that we use to distract us from truth and hinder our wholeness in Christ.

*"If you declare with your mouth, 'Jesus is Lord,' and believe in your heart that God raised him for the dead, you will be saved. For it is with your heart that you believe and are justified, and it is with your mouth that you profess your faith and are saved. As Scripture says, 'Anyone who believes in him will never be put to shame.' For there is no difference between Jew and Gentile-the same Lord is Lord of all and richly blesses all who call on him, for, 'Everyone who calls on the name of the Lord will be saved.'"*
*-Romans 10:9-13*

Thus, being healed and whole comes first from a change in heart position, truly believing that Jesus Christ is the only way of being saved. This frees us from all sin and bondage to soul ties. Through the acceptance of Jesus Christ, we have the authority and privilege for all soul ties to be severed. Jesus Christ paid the cost for all sin, including that which our souls have been and are currently tied to.

*How Do You Know When You're Healed/Whole?*

**We are healed and whole when our obedience to God is our life priority.** We are no longer slaves to our flesh but slaves of righteousness. We are no longer bound to the opinions of others nor does our flesh rule us. We openly and confidently choose God's ways over our own instant, fleshly impulses. For example, when our flesh desires to overspend when God has explicitly told us to have self-control and save, we obey. When we want to be validated by someone because we are feeling insecure, instead we open up our Bibles for the Word of God or pray that God will continue to change our heart position.

Being healed and whole is not a snap of the fingers with perfection as the end result. Being healed and whole is intentionally choosing righteousness and holiness because God is worthy. We offer our bodies as living sacrifices because it is our reasonable service to do so (Romans 12:1-2).

*"Live as free people, but do not use your freedom as a cover-up for evil; live as God's slaves."*
*-1 Peter 2:16*

*"Now the Lord is the Spirit and where the Spirit of the Lord is, there is freedom. And we all, who with unveiled faces contemplate the Lord's glory, are being transformed into His image with ever-increasing glory, which comes from the Lord, who is the Spirit."*
*-2 Corinthians 3:17-18*

**We are healed and whole when holiness is our motivation.** *"As obedient children, do not conform to the evil desires you had when you lived in ignorance. But just as he who called you is holy, so be holy in all you do; for it is written: 'Be holy, because I am holy'"* (1 Peter 1:14-16).

*"Therefore, rid yourselves of all malice and all deceit, hypocrisy, envy, slander of every kind. Like newborn babies, crave pure spiritual milk, so that by it you may grow up in your salvation, now that you have tasted that the Lord is good. As you come to*

*him, the living Stone - rejected by humans but chosen by God and precious to him - you also, like living stones, are being built into a spiritual house to be a holy priesthood, offering spiritual sacrifices acceptable to God through Jesus Christ." -1 Peter 2:1-5*

### How Do You Know That You're on the Right Path, That You're Doing What You're Supposed to Be Doing to Sever Your Soul Ties?

Following the Lord's peace in your heart is the answer. Severing soul ties is a very frustrating and messy situation. God has provided Jesus Christ to be the direct atoning sacrifice for your sin (soul ties), but the consequences that follow your engagement to the soul ties will take time to rid yourself of. Get quiet before the Lord. He may not speak right now or even in a few months, but if you stay steady with Him, He will begin to reveal His plans and ways.

My steady and continued obedience did the most benefit for severing my soul ties completely. I had to say no to my flesh while backing that choice with my physical actions. If I was making the wrong choice, I **immediately** lacked peace. I would become frustrated, angry, and disgusted with my actions.

If we are spiritually aware enough to feel conviction when making consistent sinful decisions, we are also spiritually aware enough to know when God is saying yes (peace) and no (heart torment and frustration). Don't operate in confusion. *"If any of you lacks wisdom, you should ask God, who gives generously to all without finding fault, and it will be given to you"* (James 1:5).

*"If I speak in the tongues of men or of angels, but do not have love, I am only a resounding gong or a clanging cymbal. If I have the gift of prophecy and can fathom all mysteries and all knowledge, and if I have a faith that can move mountains, but do not have love, I am nothing. If I give all I possess to the poor and give over my body to hardship that I may boast, but do not have love, I gain nothing. Love is patient, love is kind. It does not envy, it does not boast, it is not proud. It does not dishonor others, it is not self-seeking, it is not easily angered, it keeps no record of wrongs. Love does not delight in evil but rejoices with the truth. It always protects, always trusts, always hopes, always perseveres. Love never fails. But where there are prophecies, they will cease; where there are tongues, they will be stilled; where there is knowledge, it will pass away. For we know in part, and we prophesy in part, but when completeness comes, what is in part disappears. When I was a child, I talked like a child, I thought like a child, I reasoned like a child. When I become a man, I put the ways of childhood behind me. For now we see only a reflection as in a mirror; then we shall see face to face. Now I know in part; then I shall know fully, even as I am fully known. And now these three remain: faith, hope, and love. But the greatest of these is love."*
*-1 Corinthians 13:1-13*

When our hearts reflect the love of God and we truly delight in it, we are healed and whole. Our old man and its associated behaviors no longer matter because we desire the purification of love to take over our souls. Your soul no longer has room to be tied when it is overcome with God's love, as described in the Scripture above.

Again, this is a reflection of your heart's position. The greatest of all things is love. When it has truly overtaken us, as God views it and states in His Word, there is no question that we are on the right path. We are now in God's Will, being tied to Godly soul ties and severed from ungodly soul ties.

*"Therefore, as God's chosen people, holy and dearly loved, clothe yourselves with compassion, kindness, humility, gentleness and patience." -Colossians 3:12*

*"For God did not call us to be impure, but to live a holy life." -1 Thessalonians 4:7*

*"Do not be anxious about anything, but in every situation, by prayer and petition, with thanksgiving, present your requests to God. And the peace of God, which transcends all understanding, will guard your hearts and your minds in Christ Jesus. Finally, brothers and sisters, whatever is true, whatever is noble, whatever is right, whatever is pure, whatever is lovely, whatever is admirable - if anything is excellent or praiseworthy - think about such things. Whatever you have learned or received or heard from me, or seen in me - put it into practice. And the God of peace will be with you." -Philippians 4:6-9*

## Chapter 16: Can God Really Deliver Me? Will My Obedience Be Worth It?

The answer is yes. This chapter is dedicated to the doubters of God's goodness. I write as a witness and a repentant doubter. I, too, thought my sin was above His ability to deliver me. I also wondered if being obedient would be worth discontinuing my sin. In this doubt, I spent about eight years running away from God and running in circles.

If I can be honest, I thought I could deliver myself. I thought that submitting to void fillers, or ungodly soul ties, would actually make me whole. I thought that if I could only get my hair just as he liked, be present in the right situation so he could notice me, get this position so I could become the self-made woman I had been raised to be, or manipulate a situation so I could continue on cue with my life goals, then I was actually going to be happy.

Unfortunately, happiness is just a temporary feeling ruled by the impulses of the flesh. My soul was seeking a joy that is only found in God. The ability to deliver myself was a lie supported by the enemy. The devil wants us to remain in a matrix of confusion so that we are forever tied to him instead of coming into the knowledge of the Truth and receiving God's purpose for our lives.

Let me tell you how I started to experience true deliverance. See, you can't be around God's Word and His presence for too long before it starts to stick to you. This is what happened to me. No matter how much I desired to stay at my ex's house, the Lord would call me away and into quiet time with Him. Whether alone in my car, in my apartment, or participating in certain ministries at my church, the more I became involved with Him, the more I began to hate the things He hated. This included wasting time with people and circumstances that He never intended for my life (severing soul ties). I began to choose Him over and over again (deliverance).

My peak experience in realizing how submitted I was to God (choosing Him over my flesh) was after an episode of almost falling back into a sexual sin. I immediately stopped and ran out of the house to drive back to my apartment. By the time I stepped into my living room, I was on the floor crying. I felt as if I had been cheating on my husband. I felt the most intense remorse. At that moment, I truly felt the 1 Corinthians 13 love that He declared in His Word. I had been cheating on my husband. *"For your Maker is your husband - the Lord Almighty is His name - the Holy One of Israel is your Redeemer; He is called the God of all the earth"* (Isaiah 54:5). At that moment, I received every sense of His love that I could possibly understand, emotionally and spiritually. I had a desire to be delivered by God, and I knew that obedience was my only way of doing so.

Deliverance is real once you realize the extent of God's love for you. A simplified representation of this is how we get butterflies when someone of the opposite sex declares their love for us, maybe with the showing of a gift. Well, that's what I finally felt and understood. I was enamored by the showing of His love for me, a gift that I had been rejecting but could now see and appreciate. God attempts to give us His sweet gifts, but we often reject them. In this case, I am referring to His gifts of deliverance and salvation from every sin and ungodly soul tie. We've bought into the lie that deliverance is meeting certain stipulations, such as being completely separated from the sin that we struggle with, going to church certain days of the week, being involved with certain ministries, or just being all-around perfect. Deliverance is not perfection and does not involve following a formula. Deliverance is the continuous reliance on our God for righteousness and involves making active decisions to be righteous through the authority and power given to us by God.

It disgusted me to think about running back to the sexual immorality and impurity that had plagued my body, mind, and spirit for far too long. From someone who once thought that God "would have to just deal with me" in my sin and bless me anyway, I now had the desire to throw away everything (including relations and a relationship) to do exactly what He wanted of me. At that moment, I knew I was delivered and my obedience was worth it.

Again, I am no special person. I'm just someone who said yes to God's Will and Way for my life. If He did it for me, He can certainly do it for you. He delivered me from almost twelve years of sexual immorality and impurity that led to every act of the flesh. I've been "clean" now for about five years, but it is never easy. The enemy roams around like a roaring lion, but the truth of the matter is that God lives within me and gives me the authority to overcome the enemy's tactics. We have a daily choice to choose God. I am delivered from my past issues because I choose to allow God to reign in authority and power over the circumstances and issues that the enemy likes to throw in my face or tempt me with.

So why is obedience worth it? It's worth it because we receive a gift of promise.

*In his great mercy he has given us new birth into a living hope through the resurrection of Jesus Christ from the dead, and into an inheritance that can never perish, spoil or fade. This inheritance is kept in heaven for you, who through faith are shielded by God's power until the coming of the salvation that is ready to be revealed in the last time. In all this you greatly rejoice, though now for a little while you may have had to suffer grief in all kinds of trials. These have come so that the proven genuineness of your faith—of greater worth than gold, which perishes even though refined by fire—may result in praise, glory and honor when Jesus Christ is revealed. Though you have not seen him, you love him; and even though you do not see him now, you believe in him and are filled with an inexpressible and glorious joy, for you are receiving the end result of your faith, the salvation of your souls." -1 Peter 1:3-9*

It's worth it because I would have never been renewed in my mind and would have continued to partake in sin. I would have never been able to think clearly or see and do the visions God had for me all along. My life would never have been as fulfilling as it is now.

For those of you who are lost, not knowing what you should be doing in this very moment or where your life fits in this world, I guarantee you that you can't see it because you're bogged down with ungodly soul ties. God will never be able to fully unpack your destiny when you're spiritually stuffed with junk that is not of Him, period. Your purpose is waiting to be revealed as soon as you offload and rid yourself of those soul ties that are stifling you. God has called you to start, stay consistent in, and complete your process of "Severing Soul Ties!"

*Prayer*

Heavenly Father, I pray right now asking for a supernatural closeness from You to inhabit Your children who have read this book. I pray that the words You have inspired will convict them to recognize the things, circumstances, and soul ties in their lives that have kept them stifled for far too long. We have so many parts of the Body of Christ that are missing in this world because they have cut themselves off. I pray in the name of Jesus that You will regenerate them to what You have called them to be in this world. I pray for deliverance over their minds, bodies, and spirits. I pray they will see that being obedient to You is so worth it. In Jesus' name we pray, amen.

*"Therefore we do not lose heart. Though outwardly we are wasting away, yet inwardly we are being renewed day by day. For our light and momentary troubles are achieving for us an eternal glory that far outweighs them all. So we fix our eyes not on what is seen, but on what is unseen, since what is seen is temporary, but what is unseen is eternal." -2 Corinthians 4:16-18*

*"Not that I have already obtained all this, or have already arrived at my goal, but I press on to take hold of that for which Christ Jesus told hold of me. Brothers and sisters, I do not consider myself yet to have taken hold of it. But one thing I do: Forgetting what is behind and straining toward what is ahead, I press on toward the goal to win the prize for which God has called me heavenward in Christ Jesus." -Philippians 3:12-14*

## "Severing Soul Ties" Definitions

debauchery: excessive indulgence in sensual pleasures

discord: disagreement between people

dissensions: disagreement that leads to discord

drunkenness: the state of being intoxicated; intoxication

envy: a feeling of discontented or resentful longing aroused by someone else's possessions, qualities, or luck; a desire to have a quality, possession, or other desirable attribute belonging to (someone else).

factions: a state of conflict within an organization; dissension

fits of rage: violent and uncontrolled anger

hatred: intense dislike or ill will

idolatry: worship of idols; extreme admiration, love, or reverence for something or someone

impurity: the quality or condition of being impure; synonyms are adulteration, debasement, degradation, corruption

jealousy: the state of feeling of being jealous; synonymous with envy and covetousness orgies: a wild party, especially one involving excessive drinking and unrestrained sexual activity

selfish ambition: self-seeking; looking out for one's own interest instead of the interest of others

witchcraft: the practice of magic, especially black magic; the use of spells and the invocation of spirits